"NULLI SECUNDUS"

The History

— of the —

2nd Light Horse Regiment

Australian Imperial Force

August 1914—April 1919

BY

Lieut-Colonel G. H. BOURNE, D.S.O.

WITH AN INTRODUCTION

BY

Lieut. General SIR HARRY CHAUVEL, G.C.M.G., K.C.B.

The Naval & Military Press Ltd

Published by
The Naval & Military Press Ltd
5 Riverside, Brambleside, Bellbrook
Industrial Estate, Uckfield, East Sussex,
TN22 1QQ England
Tel: +44 (0) 1825 749494
Fax: +44 (0) 1825 765701
www.naval-military-press.com
www.military-genealogy.com
www.militarymaproom.com

Dedication

Dedicated to the Memory

of those Gallant Comrades,

who sailed away with us,

but did not return.

*In reprinting in facsimile from the original, any imperfections are inevitably reproduced
and the quality may fall short of modern type and cartographic standards.*

FOREWORD

THIS BOOK is an amplification of the Regimental War Diary. In addition, the author acknowledges with sincere thanks, the assistance given by Colonel R. M. Stodart V.D., Major G. Birkbeck, D.S.O., and Lieut. H. A. Weller.

To Capt. H. S. Gullett, the Official Historian, whose excellent volume throws light on many operations, and reveals, at last, the truth, the author and the whole of the 2nd L.H. Regiment are deeply indebted. He writes of us—"Few Regiments did as well as the Second and none better."

GEO. H. BOURNE,

Lieut.-Colonel

CONTENTS

ILLUSTRATIONS

INTRODUCTION.

಄

IMPERIAL GENERAL STAFF
(AUSTRALIAN SECTION)

Army Headquarters
Victoria Barracks
                                         Melbourne, 17th November, 1926

IT gives me great pleasure to write a few words of introduction to the History of the 2nd Light Horse Regiment during the Great War of 1914-18,, more particularly as this Regiment is the direct representative to-day of the Queensland Mounted Infantry, a Regiment which I joined as a subaltern thirty-six years ago and served with for many years, both in peace and during the South African War.

Under the command of Lieutenant-Colonel R. M. Stodart, the 2nd Light Horse, included in the 1st Light Horse Brigade, came under my command in the late war in Maadi, Egypt, in December, 1914, and, except for a few months when I commanded an Infantry Division, it served under my command during the whole war.

The reputation gained by the Queensland Mounted Infantry on the fields of Sunnyside, Kimberley, Paardeberg and Diamond Hill was more than maintained by the 2nd Light Horse during the Great War, whether charging from Quinn's Post, fighting a rear-guard action at Romani, attacking at Magdhaba or holding at all costs its surrounded positions at Abu Tellul.

On Gallipoli it fell to its lot immediately on arrival to hold the most difficult part of the whole Anzac line, at Quinn's Post, and finally to attack from that Post during the Battle of Sari Bair, an attack which I think has few parallels in history. Later, under Lieutenant-Colonel (now Major-General Sir William) Glasgow, it took part in all subsequent operations at Anzac.

Under Lieutenant-Colonel G. H. Bourne, the Regiment took a prominent part in all the successful operations in Sinai and Palestine. At Romani it was undoubtedly the stubborn resistance of the Regiments of the 1st Light Horse Brigade (the 1st, 2nd and 3rd Light Horse) against the Turkish attack during night of the 3rd/4th August, 1916, and their skilful delaying action on the morning of the 4th which won the Battle, thereby changing the whole phase of that campaign from an offensive to a defensive one, which culminated in the conquest of Syria and the elimination of Germany's allies from the War.

In the Jordan Valley early in the summer of 1918, the Regiment bore the brunt of two Turkish attacks, at Ghoranieh, and Abu Tellul. In the latter action the gallant resistance of is posts, surrounded on all sides as they were by the enemy, together with the spirited counter-attack of the 1st Light Horse Regiment, saved what might easily have been a very serious situation on the right of our lines.

I commend this History to the people of Australia and particularly to those of Queensland, of whose horsemen the members of the Regiment were so typical.

                           HARRY CHAUVEL,
                               Lieutenant-General
            late Commanding the Desert Mounted Corps.

CHAPTER I.

FORMATION OF THE FIRST EXPEDITIONARY FORCE

DURING the last few days of July 1914 Australia, in common with the rest of the civilised world, watched the momentous events in Europe with bated breath. For those of us who were on the Active List of the Commonwealth Military Forces, those events had, of course, a vital interest. Little did we think in those days, that huge demands would subsequently be made on others, outside the C.M.F.

Would Great Britain go to war? Where would we be employed? Could we reach the main theatre of war in time? These were questions asked or pondered many times a day. The first was definitely answered for us on August 4, and mobilisation immediately began.

Under the Compulsory Service Act of 1911 members of the C.M.F. are liable only for Home Defence; so that, in spite of the fact that in this case, the obvious and only way to defend the home was to seek the enemy in his home and cripple him, an entirely new force for service overseas, had to be organised. This Expeditionary Force was enlisted as the Australian Imperial Force. It originally consisted of one Infantry Division, complete with Artillery and Divisional Cavalry, etc., and one Light Horse Brigade. The latter was temporarily placed under the command of Lieut-Colonel J. K. Forsyth. The Regiments comprising the Brigade were—

    1st Light Horse Regiment (from 2nd Military District)
    2nd Light Horse Regiment (form 1st Military District)
    3rd Light Horse Regiment (from 4th and 6th Military District)

The Brigade Headquarters, Signal Troop, etc., were raised in the 3rd Military District.

Lieut-Colonel R. M. Stodart was appointed to Command the 2nd. Light Horse Regiment on August 18, 1914. He immediately set about selecting his Regimental Officers from the long list of applications; and the following were duly gazetted. Regimental Staff—

    Commanding Officer .. .. Lieut-Colonel R. M. Stodart
    Second-in-Command .. .. .. Major T. W. Glasgow, D.S.O.
    Adjutant .. .. Capt. F. T. H. Goucher
    Quartermaster .. .. Hon. Lieut. Chas Trotter
    Medical Officer .. .. Capt. G. W. Macartney
    Veterinary Officer .. .. Capt. R. M. Hore
    Chaplain .. .. Rev. Geo. Green, M.A.

"A" Squadron—

Major T. J. Logan	Lieut. H. Hinton.
Capt. W. E. Markwell	Lieut. T. McSharry.
Lieut. H. J. Tiddy	Lieut. W. A. B. Steele.

COLONEL R. M. STODART, V.D.
who formed the Regiment and Commanded it—August, 1914 to Sept., 1915

"B" Squadron—

Major G. H. Bourne.	Lieut. A. Chisholm.
Capt. A. W. Nash	Lieut. M. Shanahan.
Lieut. A. F. Chambers.	Lieut. J. Burge.

"C" Squadron—

Major D. M. L. Graham.	Lieut. P. Potts.
Capt. G. Birkbeck.	Lieut. A. B. Steele
Lieut A. J. Ogilvy	Lieut. S. H. Worthington.

Machine Gun Section—Lieut. A. Martin.

"A" Squadron was enlisted mainly from the Moreton and Logan and Lockyer districts. "B" Squadron from Darling Downs and Burnett districts and Central Queensland; and "C" Squadron from North Queensland and the Northern Rivers of New South Wales.

The appeals for men met with a ready response. Men representing every walk of life rolled up. Most had had service or were serving, in the C.M.F., some had had previous active service, some were discharged Imperial soldiers, some had had no training whatever. Eleven Officers, holding commissions in the C.M.F., but for whom there were at the time no vacancies in the A.I.F. relinquished their commissions temporarily and joined as privates, in order to have the honour of being in the First Expeditionary Force. Men were so plentiful that the standard of physical fitness and efficiency was high; and we had every reason to be proud of the Regiment that later on, sailed from Pinkenba.

There was much to be done however, before we were ready to embark. The men were posted to troops which comprised, as far as possible, men from the same locality, and permanent sections were formed almost invariably of four mates, or men who quickly became mates. Once organised into troops there was some appearance of order; each man knew at least, who his leader was, and from whom he could obtain much needed information.

The extraordinary pressure of work on the A and I Staff at this time naturally affected us considerably. To begin with, Permanent Instructors were at a premium. All Officers however, had been on the active list of the C.M.F., and were thoroughly up-to-date in matters of training. They were ably assisted by Squadron-Sergt.-Majors, F. J. Hockey, W. J. Brown and John Wasson—old soldiers all—so we rapidly progressed from Squad drill to Troop drill, from rifle exercises and preliminary musketry training to the Rifle Range; and so on. A little later Sergt-Major Kerr was posted from the Instrl. Staff to the Regiment as Regimental Sergt.-Major. He did much for the efficiency of the Regiment. We suffered our first serious casualty when he contracted typhoid fever, of which he died a few days after we sailed. He was succeeded by Sergt.-Major F. J. Hockey; Sergt.-Major Atkinson being appointed to "A" Squadron.

It was a red letter day when our uniforms came along. Hitherto our clothes had been decidedly mixed. Even the few original uniforms brought to camp presented endless variety, but there were in addition, bowler hats, panamas, straw boaters, felt hats, caps, etc., etc., on each parade. In our uniforms, when the old hands had initiated us, we at least felt that we looked like soldiers. Equipment came in dribs and drabs; to the dismay of Quartermaster-Sergeants, and amusement of the men who thought "Saddlery sets, complete" rather a Chinese puzzle, and "Buckets, water, canvas" an upside-down way of expressing things. The importance of the "Disc. identity with cord" was impressed on all; bringing home the grim reality of the job we were undertaking.

The most promising men were now selected as N'C.O.'s, and, as behoves the "Backbone of the Army" henceforth they were of great service in training, organising, etc.

The following are the senior N.C.O's who left Brisbane with the Regiment—

Staff. R.S.M. Hockey; R.Q.M.S. Norris; F.Q.M.S. Dunlop; O.R.S. McLennan; Signal-Sergt. Peterson; Trumpeter-Sergt Radford; Saddler-Sergt Rafter; Sergt-Cook Parker; Transport-Sergt. Uhlman.

"A" Squadron. S.S.M. Atkinson; S.Q.M.S. Power; Sergeants Ruddle, Ward, Wright, Turley, Lewis, Foreman, Barry and Galloway; and Farrier-Sergt. Pickering.

"B" Squadron. S.S.M. Brown; S.Q.M.S. Cartwright; Sergeants Brett, Willott, Smith, Curtis, Jones, Glasgow, Crain and Simkin; Farrier-sergt. Molesworth.

"C" Squadron. S.S.M. Wasson; S.Q.M.S. Gee; Sergeants Fanning, Mulherin, Oswin, Wade, Bruce, Ellwood, Tulk and Taylor; Farrier-Sergt Cheffins.

Machine Gun Section. Sergt. Williams.

Signallers, Transport-drivers, Cooks, Farriers, Saddlers, and that most indispensable adjunct of a modern army, the Sanitation Squad, were now appointed and with the exception of the tradesmen, had to undergo intensive training in their duties. The Signallers in particular, having undertaken entirely new duties and most important work, put in many hours a day at it under Signal-Sergeant Peterson, and became very efficient.

About September 10 we drew our first horses from the Remount Section and this gave us a new and very keen interest. Many men brought their horses with them; very good sorts, invariably, and these were purchased by the Remount Officer, and issued to their previous owners. A large proportion of those supplied by the Government, however, were unbroken. These were quickly taken in hand by a most capable squad of thoroughly experienced trainers; foremost among who were "Tiny" Carlyon, "Darky" Easton, Tom O'Hagan, Ernie Smith, "Bluey" Messer, Paddy Linnan. There was no lack of youthful aspirants to achieve reputations as buck-jump riders, so the older hands had all the assistance they required. The first mounted parade was now looked forward to, but before that was held, most of us had to pass a riding test. It produced some most amusing results, and eliminated many who had obviously joined the Light Horse for the sole reason that they were "too tired" to enlist in the Infantry. These men were transferred to our friends the 9th Infantry Battalion, and no doubt became useful Infantrymen.

On September 16 we had our first mounted Ceremonial parade, the

Regiment being inspected at Enoggera by the Governor-General—H. E. Sir Ronald Munro Ferguson. On 20th we marched through Brisbane, the Acting State Governor, Sir Arthur Morgan, taking the salute at the Town Hall. The horses were still very raw and many of us had an exciting time endeavouring to conform to the traffic regulations.

At length the order to embark came (there had been rumours of course for days before.)

On the afternoon of September 22, "C" Squadron moved to Pinkenba wharf; the remainder of the Regiment left Enoggera at 2.30 a.m. and arrived at Pinkenba at daylight. The greatest secrecy had been observed as to to exact date of sailing, and this, our first of very many night marches, was undertaken with that end. The ship allotted to us was the "Star of England," 8000 tons, commanded by Capt. Ullyat. For official purposes she was designated the "A. 14." She was a cargo boat, built for the frozen meat trade, etc. Horse stalls had been erected on all decks that could be sufficiently ventilated. Our first job was to get the horses on board. In this we greatly appreciated the assistance of several men who had formerly been engaged in shiping horses to India. The less experienced among us soon copied their methods, and as the whole loading operations was under control of our energetic Second-in-Command, all the horses were soon on board, and were snugly stalled and feeding. Packing saddles in saddlerooms, kits and quarter-masters' stores in the hold, etc., occupied the rest of the morning. By noon we were saying a last farewell to our friends on the wharf, and at 1 p.m. we sailed; a confident and happy (if serious) party.

CHAPTER II

THE VOYAGE

ON September 25, 1914, the Regiment sailed from Moreton Bay and many eyes gazed back at receding shores thinking of home and friends and what the future held in store. It was the first sea trip of a great majority and for a few days "mal de mer" rather interfered with the routine of work, always severe the first week at sea with some hundreds of horses stowed away between decks. However, we were off! joyously off! to do our share in keeping the old flag flying; and buoyant spirits make light of daily worries and look forward to the time when the voyage over, we would all be striking a blow for our glorious Empire.

However, the best laid schemes "gang aft aglee" and at Wilson's Promontory the cruiser Melbourne picked us up and we found that the presence of "Schornhorst" and "Gneisnau" of the German Pacific Fleet had caused a variation of sailing orders and disembarkation was to take place at Melbourne.

The Regiment left the ship at Williamstown and proceeded to the Showgrounds where it remained till October 20.

Everything possible to make things comfortable was done there both by the Showground Committee and the 3rd District staff. The C./O. had correspondence both with Mr. Fisher, Prime Minister, and Mr. Pearce, Minister for Defence, endeavouring to secure permission to wear the Emu Plume and this culminated during a visit to the camp by these gentlemen who after talking the matter over announced on parade that the plume might be worn and thus was settled for all time the distinguishing badge of the Australian Light Horse, which Queenslanders had made famous on many fields during the war in South Africa. This concession was greatly appreciated by all ranks.

During the stay in Victoria everything was done to bring about a spirit of camaraderie amongst the men. The 4th L.H. (Vic.) marched in and met us, the two regiments mingling and becoming acquainted. Advantage also was taken of the break to remedy such little defects on the "Star of England" as had become apparent on the voyage down the coast and when we re-embarked at Williamstown on October 20 it was an improved and less crowded ship that greeted us, Lieut Worthington and the transport horses being transferred to the "Anglo-Egyptian."

Without incident we reached Albany on October 26 where the fleet collected and took in water etc., eventually sailing on November 1, consisting of 40 large transports adequately escorted by British and Japanese ships of war.

It was a grand sight to see this array stretching away in three long lines to the horizon—one never tired of looking across the restless ocean and feeling proud of the race which could transport from one side of

Typical Village in the Nile Valley

the globe to the other, so many ships, so many men, so soon after Declaration of War with a Nation which claimed to be the most powerful under the sun.

But the "Emden" was near ! This enemy cruiser had done much damage in the Eastern Seas and such a fleet as ours might disclose its presence by empty cases etc., thrown overboard, indeed the Captain of H.M.S. "Hampshire" had recently sent us all a message reminding us that we were not engaged on a "paper chase." Orders were therefore issued that no boxes, paper, etc., were to be thrown overboard to disclose the convoy's position.

On November 9 we were all surprised to see the Sydney, which occupied a station on our port side, suddenly turn and steam full speed out of sight in the direction of the Cocos Islands, then about 50 miles away. She went off at 7 a.m. and at 11 a.m. we received word that she had met and destroyed the famous "Emden." Needless to say we were all very jubilant at the news and regretted that the "scrap" had not occurred in full view of the fleet.

We anchored off Colombo on 15th, and sailed again on 17th; the New Zealanders only, being allowed ashore.

On November 28 we learned by wireless that we had declared war on Turkey and that Egypt not France was to be our destination for the present.

The monotony of the voyage through the Red Sea was enlivened by a court case in which the ship's newspaper was sued for damages. This occasioned much merriment and helped to while away the long hours. The Suez Canal was entered at 3 p.m. on December 2nd and every inch of it well protected by British Indian troops. It was our first sight of Sikh and Gurkha and much curiosity was displayed both by them and us. After a few hours stay at Port Said we proceeded on to Alexandria where our disembarkation was completed by 2 p.m. on December 9 the Regiment having been in the ship for 70 days.

The long and tedious trip across was relieved by a weekly sports day and a weekly concert, both much appreciated by all ranks. Drill and training was carried on continuously—physical exercises, rifle drill and lectures being carried out together with stable duties which occupy so much of a mounted man's time. It was truly wonderful how well the animals stood the journey and the excellent condition in which they arrived with but two or three casualties.

We were much indebted to our genial Master for helping to pass the voyage absolutely devoid of friction and Capt. Ulyatt will not be forgotten by the original members of the 2nd. Light Horse (A.I.F.) who left their mark of appreciation on the vessel in the form of a ship's bell suitably inscribed..

CHAPTER III

EGYPT

WE berthed at daylight. The up-to-date equipment of the quays was an eye opener to most of us. A start was soon made to unload the horses and get them into the trucks which were drawn up ready, almost alongside the ship. Most of the horses gave no trouble—but a few outlaws (notably Billy the Bastard—who was afterwards to become famous in the Regiment) made a name for themselves. At 4 p.m. the first train with half the Regiment and 230 horses, left for Cairo. About an hour later a second train left with the balance of the Regiment. The journey to Cairo took five hours. Strange to say it was raining fairly heavily when we arrived. So little provision is made for storm water there that the streets were turned into a quagmire. Leading our horses (they were too weak to ride after that long journey) we marched on foot to Ma'adi, guided by a native policeman. We were fully equipped and each man led one or two horses. The distance was only about 9 miles—but by the time we reached our destination, shortly before dawn—we estimated it at 20 miles at least.

There were not nearly enough tents—camp equipment not having arrived from England—but we spent the next week erecting what tents could be collected, and forming a camp neat enough to please the most particular of inspecting officers.

Horses were given daily exercise by being led over the Desert for a couple of hours. They did not take too kindly to the Egyptian rations. The "tibben" (chaffed rice straw) supplied by the contractors was full of dirt —though it improved later.

Training during the first ten days, consisted of dismounted drill. There was great rivalry between the three Regiments of the Brigade, in the turning out of Brigade Guards; and it was not long before these would have done credit to a regular Regiment

On December 18 our first mounted parade in Egypt was held and the horses showed that they had quite recovered their land legs—several having "foals."

About this time Colonel H. G. Chauvel arrived from England and assumed command of the Brigade.

The Sultan of Egypt being a pro-Turk, was deposed by the British Government. A Protectorate was established and a new Sultan proclaimed. In order to impress on the native population that we were in a position to enforce this if necessary, the whole of the British troops available marched through Cairo on December 23. This demonstration had the desired effect and the change of Government passed off without incident.

Mounted training was now begun in earnest—the Desert and the broken country in the vicinity of the Mokattam Hills being very suitable. Signallers became proficient with the Helio. Stretcher bearers were trained—a sanitary squad formed etc. etc. We also fired a musketry course here.

There was not much in the way of comfort for the men as the camp-equipment was very limited—and no army canteens had been established. Ma'adi however is an English suburb—beautifully laid out—and the residents spared themselves no trouble on our behalf. Many threw open their homes, to both officers and men. Ladies supplied stationery, periodicals etc for a writing room; and personally managed a dry canteen. The many acts of kindness by the people of Ma'adi were much appreciated by all ranks.

On January 30 however, we were moved from Ma'adi to Heliopolis.

This was the result of re-organisation, by which the 1st L.H. Brigade became part of the New Zealand and Australian Division, commanded by Major-General Sir Alex. Godley. Our future training was in conjunction with the other units of that Division—chiefly the New Zealand Mounted Rifles, with whom we were so closely associated later.

During January, though we knew nothing of it, a Turkish Army Corps had been steadily advancing from Bueersheba to attack the Suez Canal.

The force was well equipped with guns and carried boats and pontoons, the transport of which across the desert of Sinai was an undertaking which compelled our admiration when 15 months later we traversed the same country. The attack was launched on the night of February 1 and was completely repulsed by the posts guarding the Canal. Some New Zealanders were employed in this action and we were disappointed that they should have received their baptism of fire before we did.

All day and every day was spent in the Desert—protection on the move —at rest—attack and defence—night operations, etc., etc.—till we could have found "Tower No. 3" and the "Virgin's Breasts" and other land marks, blindfolded. We were really becoming a highly efficient force, and were looking forward to our active employment in Europe.

From Brigade schemes we progressed to Divisional manoeuvres and after each operation, the work was criticised by senior officers.

Two notable variations in our training were—practising swimming the horses over the Nile at the Barrage, on an endless rope; and ferrying them across in native barges, at Helouan. These operations were carried out without accident. They certainly encouraged the idea which had gained currency after our inspection by Sir Ian Hamilton in March, that we were to be employed in Southern Europe and "on the Plains of Hungary."

While on the Helouan operations, all ranks were given the opportunity to visit the wonderful "Tombs of Sakhara." Small parties, too, managed to get short leave to visit Luxor and see the famous temples there, the ancient city of Thebes, the Colossi of Memnon, Tombs of the Kings, etc.

CHAPTER IV.

GALLIPOLI

APRIL 25, 1915, a date of which future generations of Australians will justly be proud, found the 1st L.H. Brigade, including the 2nd Regiment at Helouan. We knew that the Infantry had sailed some days previously for an unknown destination but it was only on our return to camp at Heliopolis that we received news of the wonderful landing at Anzac. We were told that reinforcements were urgently required; and that it had been decided that the 1st L.H. Brigade and the New Zealand Mounted Rifle Brigade should leave their horses at Heliopolis and proceed to Gallipoli as Infantry as soon as the necessary equipment could be improvised, etc. Two drafts of Reinforcements had reached us, under Lieuts. Franklin and Boyd respectively. Lieuts. S. H. Worthington and A. B. Steele having been detached from the Regiment on duty. Lieut. Boyd was absorbed into "C" Squadron, Lieut. Franklin was detailed to remain in charge of the horses, with the Farriers and unabsorbed reinforcements. The Regiment at full strength, spent the next few days handing in saddlery, mounted equipment, kit, etc., and otherwise preparing for the long-looked-for move.

The first casualties from the Infantry arrived at No. 1 Australian General Hospital, Heliopolis, on May 2, and we eagerly sought out friends and endeavoured to learn from them something of the objective, the ground, the nature of the fighting, etc. Maps were at a premium. Improvised Infantry equipment was issued to us on May 7th and on the following evening we marched with packs up to Helmiah Railway station where we entrained. Reaching Alexandria on 9th we embarked on the s.s. "Devanna" with the 1st. L.H. Regiment. Our transport horses and ten saddle horses were shipped on the "Kingstonian" in charge of Captain Nash as it was anticipated we would have use for them at least, as soon as we landed.

The voyage, though full of thrills, and submarine alarms, passed without incident, and at 7 a.m. on May 12 we were trans-shipped into destroyers and from them into lighters which were towed to the beach at Anzac Cove by steam pinnaces, commanded by pink and white midshipmen, whose effiiciency and coolness seemed inconsistent with their apparent youth.

We came under fire when approaching the beach but only four men were hit. We bivouaced that night in Monash Gully.

Before dawn on the 13th the senior officers were shown round Quinn's Post with a view to taking it over from 15th Battalion which had held it so gallantly since April 29, and which was urgently in need of relief. This post, the apex of the triangle held, had the reputation of being the most vulnerable in the whole line; and the description of it, as given us by the men of the R.M.L.I. who had been supporting the 15th, was lurid enough.

The post consisted of a single line of trenches dug just on the crest of a semi-circular ridge, and was divided into six subsections. Enemy trenches

ANZAC COVE—GALLIPOLI

were only ten yards away at one point and on higher ground. The main enemy works were distant about 20 yards but were connected with our fire trench by three communication trenches which had been dug by the 15th Battalion early in May when they captured and for a short time held the enemy's front line. Two of these had been partly filled in, but that leading into No. 6 subsection was quite open except for a few sandbags which made an obstacle three feet high.

The position was commanded by the Chess Board and Dead Man's Ridge on the left and by German officers trench on the right; and so could be enfiladed from either flank at from 100 to 300 yards. Communication trenches connected the fire trenches with the water course up which all traffic to the post had to pass, but one of these, that leading into No. 5 subsection was commanded by German officers' trench and many casualties occurred in it.

At noon on May 13 we took over "Quinns"—"C" Squadron on the right, "B" Squadron on the left, "A" being in support. The 1st L.H. Regiment at the same time took over Popes—the next post on our left. The intervening ridge, "Dead Man's," was untenable to either side.

We had heard a little about Bombs, but thought that as they were employed in the Crimean War, and hardly since, they must be more or less obsolete. We were soon to be enlightened. The enemy bombed us well all the afternoon. Our trench was very wide and it was almost impossible for "Jacko" to miss dropping his handy cricket ball bombs in. We suffered a number of casualties, viz. Lieut. Hinton and Lieut Boyd and 32 men wounded, till we learned to smother the bombs, or better still to throw them back. The need for absolute silence was also impressed on us. The number of men actually in the trenches was reduced to the minimum.

Our periscopes showed us very little to our immediate front though constant watch was kept.

At dusk the firing line was strengthened but the night passed quietly. Early on the 14th the sentry group on guard at communication trench leading to No. 6 subsection, viz. Troopers Rogan, Butler and Stark, reported that a man speaking in subdued and broken English intimated that he wished to give himself up. He was brought in from the enemy trench by Major Bourne and passed to the rear. The Intelligence Staff were hopeful that others might be induced to follow, but efforts to pursuade them to do so merely attracted bombs of which we got our full issue.

On the afternoon of 14th General Birdwood visited the post and decided that, in view of the daily wastage, apart from any sorties that might be necessary, a Light Horse Regiment was not strong enough numerically to garrison the post. To our surprise we received orders to hand over to the 15th Battalion who had hardly had 24 hours rest. Our "C" Squadron under Major Graham, however, was detailed to remain on the post, to assault the enemy position during the night, to fill in the communication trenches, damage the enemy trenches and return before daylight. There was no artillery or other preparation as the attack was intended to be a surprise.

The hour ordered for the assault was 1.45 a.m. May 15, and the parties, four in number, were led by Capt Birkbeck and Lieut. Ogilvy (assaulting parties) and Major Graham and Lieut. Potts (digging parties). Several similar sorties had been made previously by the 15th Infantry, and the Turks had therefore placed machine guns on the Chess Board to the north and at German officers' trench to the south to sweep the narrow No Man's Land between the opposing trenches. Our assaulting parties had hardly mounted the parapet when they were met by showers of bombs and a tremendous volume of rifle fire. Taking up the alarm the machine guns to right and left opened on the attackers, with the result that only Lieut. Ogilvy and three men reached the enemy trench. Although the enemy retired, Lieut. Ogilvy at once realised the hopelessness of remaining in the position and he wisely ordered his men to retire through the old communication trench and to bring in the wounded. Stretcher bearers dashed out through the hail of lead, in the gallant attempts to rescue those badly hit. Those of the wounded who were able, crawled back, some over the parapet, some into the communication saps. Major Graham, seeing that the surprise attack had failed, ordered the digging parties to stand fast in Quinn's. He himself scrambled out and ran forward to help in the wounded. While so engaged this gallant officer was killed. Capt. Birkbeck and Lieut. Ogilvy were wounded, and of the 60 men who made the sortie 25 were killed and 21 wounded.

The remainder of "C" Squadron was relieved by a squadron of 3rd L.H. Regiment, and rejoined the regiment in reserve. During the following three days we were employed in digging trenches and forming a second line of defence. Though only small parties were actually in the firing line during that period we had three men killed and 19 wounded—chiefly by snipers whose operations from now on became very deadly. On May 15, Major-General Bridges commanding the 1st Australian Division was mortally wounded in Monash Valley. This was a great blow to the whole A.I.F. which he had formed and trained. Brig-Gen. Walker of 1st Infantry Brigade succeeded temporarily to the command of 1st Division.

On May 16 Captain A. Nash (2nd in Command "B" Squadron) was promoted to command "C" Squadron.

On May 19 the Turks launched an attack on the whole of the Anzac position. Increased enemy artillery activity had given some warning of this and our own Intelligence Officers seem to have obtained reliable information concerning it on 18th, as the whole garrison was ordered to be on the alert. On night 18th the Turks seemed very "windy" and their fire was heavier than usual.

The ball opened on the right section, where our positions at Lone Pine and Johnston's Jolley were heavily attacked and successfully defended. Courtney's Post, on the right of Quinn's was entered by the enemy and it was in helping to eject them that Jacka of 14th Battalion won the V.C.

The 2nd Regiment, less one squadron, was detailed as support to the 1st Regiment which was then holding Pope's Hill and which was attacked before dawn. The attack was repulsed, however, by machine gun and rifle fire.

Our "B" Squadron was attached to 15th Battalion, holding Quinn's, the defence of which had been greatly strengthened by machine guns located at Popes' Hill (under Capt. A. Martin) and Courtney's, which fired obliquely across the front of Quinn's. At this point also the enemy attack failed to survive the rifle and machine gun fire.

It was ascertained subsequently that 42,000 enemy troops took part in the attack and that they suffered 10,000 casualties. The stench which came from the narrow No Man's Land can hardly be imagined. At Quinn's corpses were heaped within three feet of our parapet and swarms of flies divided their attention between the dead bodies and our food.

On May 24th, at the request of the Turks who sent messengers protected by Red Crescent flags, an Armistice was granted for the purpose of burying the dead. Firing ceased at 7.30 a.m. Both sides furnished burying parties, and sentries were posted about midway across No Man's Land, which was ridiculously narrow at some points to prevent either side overlooking the entrenchments of the other. Our Regiment supplied 50 men under Captain Nash. Our Chaplain, Captain Green, accompanied the party and read the burial service over those of our own dead. Identity discs were collected and every effort was made to trace men who had been reported as "missing." At 4.30 p.m. the Armistice ended and the working parties returned to their respective lines. We had three men hit during the afternoon.

On May 25 we occupied Reserve Gully but had five men wounded. About mid-day H.M.S. "Triumph" was torpedoed by a German submarine just off Anzac Beach. She sank within half-an-hour. Practically the whole of her crew was saved, but the sight of this battleship, which a few minutes before had seemed so full of power, heeling over and disappearing, was depressing in the extreme to us, and no doubt was hailed with great joy by the enemy. Two days later the "Majestic" also was sunk at Helles, but of course we at Anzac did not see that. The activity of enemy submarines was responsible for the withdrawing of battleships from supporting the troops, their place being taken by destroyers.

On May 26 we took over Popes' Hill from 1st L.H. Regiment. This post was a rest, compared with the strenuous Quinn's; besides which we had now shaken down to trench duties. During the following week Major Glasgow, Capt. Martin and Lieut. Trotter were wounded and three men were killed and 12 wounded. Sniping was persistently kept up all day, though for the most part the enemy showed very little to shoot at, except periscopes. These we shattered for him regularly, and to do him justice he returned the compliment. Each night parties were employed improving the trenches.

About this time it was reported by some old miners in the 15th Battalion that the Turks were endeavouring to tunnel under Quinn's Post, and in order to construct counter-mines, men with underground experience were called for from all units. Our Regiment furnished 12 miners (from Mt. Morgan, Gympie and Charters Towers chiefly) under Sergt. Crain. These worked strenuously in their endeavours to frustrate the enemy miners and succeeded in blowing in a couple of Jacko's tunnels that had been pushed dangerously close to our trench. About mid-night on 29th, however, the Turks exploded a big mine, blowing in part of Quinn's (and incidentally blowing up Sergt. Crain though he was not badly hurt). The enemy followed up the explosion; and taking advantage of the temporary confusion, occupied part of the Post, at that time garrisoned by 13th Battalion with 15th Batalion in support. Counter attacks were at once organised and after severe fighting the Turks were ejected leaving many casualties and prisoners behind. Lieut. McSharry of our Regiment, who had been appointed Post adjutant at Quinn's, took a leading part in the counter attack. Our Regiment from its position in the adjoining Post, Popes', was able to give valuable assistance by machine gun and rifle fire.

On June 2 we were relieved at Pope's by 1st L.H. Regiment. This Post and the gully between it and Russell's Top were now definitely allotted to the 1st L.H. Brigade, the 1st, 2nd and 3rd Regiments garrisoning them in rotation—those not on the Post, acting as support. While in support we were continually employed on fatigue work, digging trenches and saps constructing the second line of defence, carrying rations, water and engineer's stores from the beach etc. All this time enemy snipers were very active and took daily toll.

On June 4 we lost one man, killed and the C.O. Lieut.-Col. Stodart and Medical Officer Capt. Macartney and one man wounded.

On June 16 we again took over Pope's and during our week's tour of duty there had been 13 casualties.

About this time a few periscope rifles were issued. They were made by the engineers on the beach. Though th credit for the idea is given to others, Trooper E. J. Ubank of our Regiment had made a rought but useful periscope rifle previously.

A very primitive trench mortar for throwing Garland Bombs was supsupplied to the Post about this time. Though it consisted of only about two feet of piping set on a stand and was fired by a small charge of powder it was fairly effective. The range was varied by increasing or reducing the charge. Birch, Tassy Smith and others who worked it, used to lob the bombs well into the enemy trenches. The Japanese bomb thrower worked from Quinn's was a much more powerful weapon and was much dreaded by the Turks—but unfortunately ammunition for it was very limited.

On June 23 we were relieved at Pope's—but our week in support finished up with a lively engagement.

The head of Monash Gully recently had been greatly strengthened by working parties from the 1st L.H. Brigade. The 3rd L.H. Regiment constructed a good and fairly well protected road (Viney's Road—named after the Adjutant of the 3rd Regiment) right up between the left of Pope's Hill and Walker's Ridge. This was ultimately connected with Walker's Ridge by Bully Beef Sap. Protecting the head of Viney's Road the 2nd Regiment had constructed a small work called, after Lieut. Hinton who was in charge of the party that built it, Hinton's Post.

There was an eerie feeling about the early part of the night—June 29-30, chiefly owing to a most uncomfortable storm. The Turks seemed jumpy; but we thought this was because they expected us to attack (our friends of 5th L.H. Regiment and 9th Infantry Battalion had made an attack on the right flank the day before and had suffered heavy casualties in doing so.) Various demonstrations along the whole front were indulged in by the Anzac troops, to add to the enemy's apparent nervousness.

MAJOR-GENERAL SIR T. W. GLASGOW, K.C.B., C.M.G., D.S.O.
Commanding Officer—September, 1915 to February, 1916

We learned years afterwards (see Bean's "Story of Anzac") that Enver Pasha had ordered a general attack for June 28 but that the attack by the 5th L.H. Regiment and 9th Battalion above referred to, upset the enemy plans, and caused a postponment for 24 hours.

Walker's Ridge, Russell's Top and the Nek were at this time held by 3rd L.H. Brigade, Popes' Post and Viney's Road by 1st L.H. Brigade while Quinn's was garrisoned by New Zealand Infantry (Auckland Battalion) and against these positions the Turks launched their attack about midnight. The 1st L.H. Regiment held Popes' with one Squadron of 3rd Regiment attached. The 2nd Regiment held the valley between Popes and Russell's Top with "B" Squadron—"A" and "C" in support. The 3rd Regiment less one Squadron was Brigade Reserve. After shelling the positions the enemy made a determined assault on the 3rd Brigade at the Nek and actually occupied some of the trenches. They were vigorously counter attacked and ejected by the 8th L.H. Regiment. Simultaneously a considerable force advanced down the valley towards Viney's Road, apparently with a view to attacking Russell's Top in flank. Supported by the 1st Regiment machine guns at Popes' which were splendidly handled by Capt. Broadbent, "B" Squadron of 2nd Regiment repulsed the enemy—D and C troops under Lieuts. Burge and Chisholm, counter attacking with the bayonet, drove the enemy right up the valley losing two men killed, and two wounded. Lt.-Corp. Warden carried in one of the latter (Cpl. Miller) who was badly hit. While Colonel Stodart was instructing Major Nash (O.C. "C" Squadron) to support "B" Squadron the latter was killed by a chance shot which also wounded his second-in-command, Capt. Birkbeck. Major Allan Nash was one of the most efficient, conscientious and respected officers in the Regiment and his loss was a serious one. Capt. F. T. Goucher (adjutant) was promoted to command "C" Squadron and Lieut. Tiddy was appointed Adjutant. Both received steps in rank.

From July 1 to 5 we were Brigade Reserve—being fully occupied during the period in heavy manual labour. The weather was very hot and there was now a good deal of sickness among the men, caused chiefly by the flies which swarmed everywhere. Though the authorities were now giving more attention to sanitation, latrine accommodation was of the crudest type and the spread of disease from that source and from the unburied dead seemed inevitable. The rations too, though ample as regards quantity, were unsuitable for the climate. Bully beef of very inferior quality, hard biscuits, cheese, semi-liquid owing to the heat, very fat bacon and the everlasting Apricot jam, which was not much more than coloured water, were far from appetising to men suffering from diarrhoea and dysentery and who were beginning to show signs of the constant strain.

On July 6 we again took over Pope's Hill—but the Regiment was so weak numerically that we had one Squadron 3rd Regiment attached. Our tour of duty was comparatively quiet as the enemy had not recovered from the severe repulse of June 30.

On July 12 the British and French made another general attack at Helles, and the Anzac troops were instructed to make feints and nightly stunts to keep the enemy nervy and prevent him from withdrawing troops from Anzac to reinforce his Helles position. The 6th and 7th L.H. Regiments made a sortie on our right flank. The Ramadan Fast began this week. Our Intelligence Officers ascertained that the enemy contemplated an attack on us on a huge scale, that he was being reinforced by 100,000 men and that gas would be used. We were therefore issued with gas helmets. Though they were of a very primitive pattern, they were reported serviceable and we practised wearing them and working in them.

We were relieved from the front line on July 14 and were in support till 29th when we again toop over Pope's. Whether in or out of the front line, the enemy took daily toll in casualties; and though we had received two drafts of reinforcements, we were reduced at this stage to 100 bayonets—hardly one man being really fit. Though hitherto all ranks had made a point of going to the beach when off duty, for a swim (that being the only way to keep even moderately clean) the heavy fatigue work, the long night watches in the Trenches and the tension generally, had so weakened the men that few had strength to walk to the beach. We had invariably "stood to arms" an hour before dawn—but during Ramadan, we stood to arms for an hour after moon-set also—with the result that even when not in the trenches men were getting very little sleep. The Medical Officers had had orders to evacuate no man who could hold a rifle. Though these had been slightly relaxed, to the credit of the men be it said, they stuck to their posts as long as humanly possible.

While we were strenuously working to dig new trenches and improve old ones, to tunnel underground, to dig sunken roads for the protection of traffic etc, the Turks were similarly employed and the fresh lines of trenches, the machine gun positions etc., which confronted us each morning were really wonderful. Our snipers had been organised early in June and we had obtained superiority of fire. Every loophole Jacko constructed was well peppered each day; and he was hard put to it to devise some material which would withstand our bullets. Camel-hair sandbags were first used— but these were shot through so often that the sand ran out and they collapsed. A few concrete loop holes were installed—evidently as an expriment. Our snipers used to aim at the sides of these with the object of getting a "cannon off the cush" or in other words a ricochet down Jacko's trench. They must have cost the enemy numerous casualties in this way, for they were all removed within a few days. Wickerwork loop holes replaced them and were much more difficult to deal with. After a while however, we learnt to cut them out with machine guns. Our supporting batteries too, gave great help. With a F.O.O in our front trench directing the shooting by telephone, shells were repeatedly put right into the loop holes.

During the last 10 days of July, our senior officers were ordered two at a time, to report to the Destroyer "Colne." They were taken up the coast as far as Suvla Bay and were ordered to study the country thoroughly with their field glasses. Rumours of a fresh offensive by the Anzac troops quickly got round—but of reliable information there was none. We did not even know at that time that New Zealand scouts had been exploring the ravines and penetrating well into the enemy's country to the north of the Anzac position. The prospects of an advance and of bringing the stalemate to an end heartened the troops, weak and thoroughly debilitated though they were; and as a result, the number of men reporting sick diminished.

The weather was now very hot. Partly owing to the fact that the General Staff was endeavouring to build up a reserve supply of fresh water, and partly because enemy shells had destroyed some of our water barges, our water ration, never liberal, was reduced to one quart per day. This was a genuine hardship. Though several wells had been sunk, the supply obtained on Gallopli itself was practically negligible. The great bulk of our drinking water was brought from Malta, pumped from ships into barges, thence into tanks on shore. It was then carried in eight gallon "fantassis" on mules to the various unit areas and issued to the troops.

During the last few days of July all troops not in the front line were engaged preparing bivouac sites in the back areas for fresh units. Thus the rumours of a big offensive by us were confirmed.

On July 31 there was severe fighting on our right flank, the Infantry pushing out and occupying a position in front of Tasmania Post. Lieut. Chambers was evacuated ill this day. Each night fresh units were now landing and were being packed into the bivouacs prepared for them. To us, now old campaigners, they seemed very raw.

On August 4, Regimental Commanders were summoned to a conference at G.H.Q. and were there given orders for their attack. Lieut-Col. Stodart having been appointed Post Commander at Quinn's and Major Glasgow holding a similar position at Pope's, Major Bourne was temporarily in command of the Regiment and attended the conference. The fact that our senior officers had been taken to spy out the land to the north of Anzac had led us to believe that we would be operating in that area, but a totally different role was assigned to us. Very briefly the outline of the plan was explained at the conference as follows:—

At 3.50 p.m. on August 6 the British would attack at Helles. At 5.30 the Australian Division at Anzac would attack Lone Pine. At 10 p.m. the New Zealand and Australian Division with attached troops—(but less the 1st and 3rd L.H. Brigades) would move by the beach north of the Anzac position and take Chunuk Bair Hill 971 and Battleship Hill.

During the night a new force would land at Suvla Bay and take Chocolate and W. Hills thus covering the left flank of the New Zealand and Australian Division, whose objectives were the key to the position. It was expected that the Suvla force would threaten the rear of the whole Turkish position.

The 3rd L.H. Brigade was to attack the Nek and "Baby 700" from Russell's Top.

The 1st L.H. Brigade was to attack the Chessboard from Popes' (by 1st L.H. Regiment) and Turkish Quinn's from Quinn's (by 2nd L.H. Regiment). The 3rd L.H. Regiment was to be Brigade Reserve. The attacks by both L.H. Brigades were intended to co-operate with the right flank of the New Zealand and Australian Division in its attacks on the objectives abovementioned. They were the keys to the whole Gallipoli area.

As a preliminary step the 2nd Regiment took over Quinn's Post on August 5, relieving the New Zealand Infantry (Auckland Battalion). We were ordered to attack in four waves of 50 men each. Reinforcements to bring us up to rather over that strength arrived on August 6. Quinn's Post had been greatly improved since we first held it. It now boasted a new fire trench and some covered support trenches. Moreover the fire trench was protected to a fair extent from bombs by the erection of wire netting screens, which from a distance resembled fowl yard fences. These screens while in position absolutely prevented egress from the trenches of the left sector. To remove them would have given positive warning to the enemy of the intended atack at that point. Major Bourne who had been made responsible for the details of the attack, therefore ordered the crust of a tunnel which had been driven from the extreme left of Quinn's, to the left front, to be broken in, to be used as a jumping off line for the left attacking party ("B" Squadron). Portion of the wire netting was prepared for removal in front of Section 4, to enable the right attacking party ("A" Squadron) to charge. This wire was left intact till shortly before the actual sortie. Arrangements were made for digging parties, under Capt. Markwell, to dig communication trenches across No Man's Land, should the attack succeed.

At the conference at G.H.Q. on August 4 the Regimental representative was told that on account of the great difficulties attached to it the attack from Quinn's would not be made until:—

1. German Officers Trench had been taken.
2. The New Zealanders had captured Chunuk Bair and were advancing against the rear of the Chess Board and Turkish Quinn's.
3. A thorough bombardment of the Chess Board and Turkish Quinn' had been carried out.

These conditions were only reasonable, as without their fulfilment the attack from Quinn's was foredoomed to be an expensive failure. As previously explained the enemy machine guns from the Chess Board and German Officers Trench absolutely commanded Quinn's and had been responsible for the annihilation of several other parties attacking thence.

The signal for the attack was to be the explosion of a big mine under Turkish Quinn's. The hour was fixed for 4.30 a.m. During the night demonstrations and heavy bombing were carried out to pin the enemy to his ground and prevent him reinforcing Chunuk Bair etc. The C.O. Lieut. Col. Stodart was to command and to proceed with the fourth line. The first second and third waves were to be led by Majors Bourne and Logan and Lieuts. Burge, Shanahan, Franklin, Chisholm, Norris and Hinton.

Shortly after 4 a.m. a Brigade message ordered Lieut.-Col. Stodart and his adjutant, Capt. Tiddy, to remain personally at Quinn's and to prepare for a counter attack by the enemy, should our attack fail. Major Bourne was therefore ordered to take Colonel Stodart's place.

We now found that the attack on German Officers Trench had failed. There was no sign of the New Zealanders on Chunuk Bair and certainly no evidence of their even threatening the Chess Board and Turkish Quinn's A few shrapnel burst over our objective—but nothing in the nature of a bombardment. Nevertheless our order to attack still held; and we waited for the explosion of the mine which was to hurl part of the enemy's front line into the air and give us at least some assistance. The mine made about as much noise as a jam tin bomb and had probably had less effect. (The engineers admitted afterwards that it had not been driven as far as had been hoped and that had they put a decent charge of T.N.T. into it, our own,

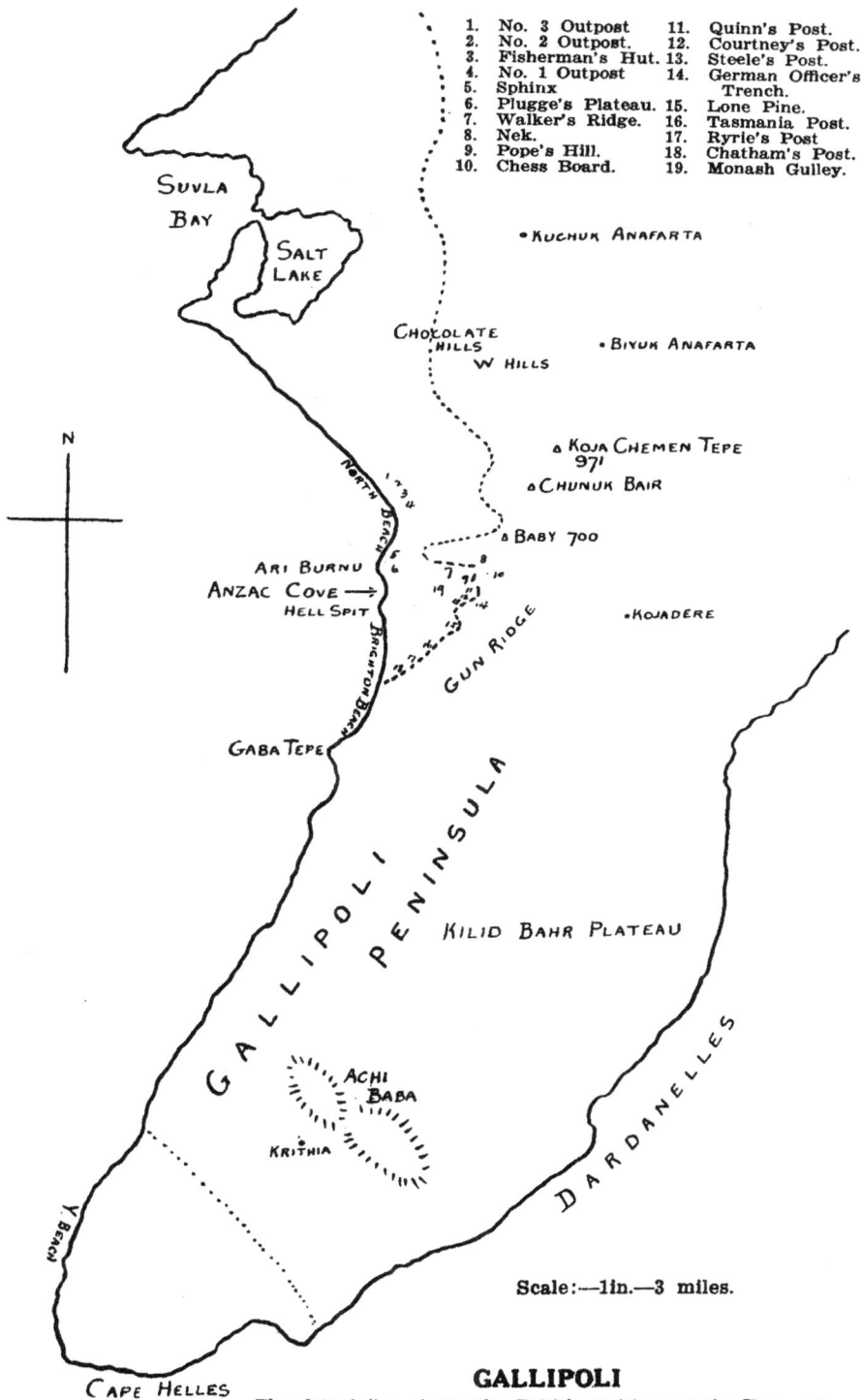

SUVLA BAY

SALT LAKE

• KUCHUK ANAFARTA

CHOCOLATE HILLS

• BIYUK ANAFARTA

W HILLS

N

North Beach

Δ KOJA CHEMEN TEPE 971'

Δ CHUNUK BAIR

Δ BABY 700

ARI BURNU

ANZAC COVE →

HELL SPIT

• KOJADERE

Brighton Beach

GUN RIDGE

GABA TEPE

GALLIPOLI PENINSULA

KILID BAHR PLATEAU

DARDANELLES

ACHI BABA

KRITHIA

Y BEACH

Scale:—1in.—3 miles.

CAPE HELLES

GALLIPOLI

The dotted line shows the British positions at the Evacuation

and not the enemy trenches, would have been demolished). Major Bourne ordered the first wave to charge. Major Logan and Lieuts. Norris and Burge gallantly led out their men amid a perfect hail of lead. Many were hit as they leapt from our trenches—some got ten yards—every man but one, was hit, most of them in a dozen places. Seeing that the enemy was so fully prepared, that the other parties, if the attack were persisted in, must be annihilated as the first was; and realising that if the whole 200 men detailed for the attack became casualties the remaining garrison at Quinn's would be powerless to resist a counter attack, Major Bourne ordered the second line to stand fast pending further orders. He then personally reported the situation to Colonel Stodart who obtained the authority of B.H.Q. to defer a further attempt. To have pressed the attack would have been futile waste of gallant lives. Already we had lost those sterling officers— Major Logan and Lieut. Burge, killed. In addition Lieut. Norris was wounded—14 other ranks killed and 36 wounded. The Regiment had made that sacrifice in an absolutely forlorn hope. Every man knew that the attack itself could not, under the circumstances, possibly have succeeded—but each was willing to make the sacrifice in order to hold a large force of the enemy in his trenches and thus assist the major operation which was proceeding on our distant left, and which we earnestly hoped was succeeding.

There was no chance whatever of stretcher bearers working in that narrow No Man's Land. Those wounded who were able to move, rolled back over our parapet. The dead we were never able to recover. Lieut. Hinton was killed while firing over the parapet to cover the withdrawal of the wounded. Throughout the morning, by firing obliquely at the Chess Board we endeavoured to repel the counter attack by the enemy against the 1st L.H. Regiment who, led by our Major Glasgow, temporarily in command, actually reached the third line of enemy trenches opposite Pope's and held them for a couple of hours. Every officer (except Major Glasgow who bore a charmed life) and almost every man, having been either killed or wounded, the 1st Regiment attacking party withdrew to Pope's with as many of their wounded as they could carry. We maintained the rifle and bomb attack throughout the day. The night was an anxious one, but though there was plently of bombing, it passed without any particular incident—the enemy being too fully occupied with the operations on our left flank and with his counter attack on Lone Pine, to counter attack us.

Operations continued at daybreak on 8th—though the enemy, apparently having realised that there could be no further serious assaults by us, was not so active and had apparently withdrawn some of his garrison for duty elsewhere. We had one man wounded. We anxiously sought news of the operations on our left and the reports received this day were most hopeful. It still looked as if we might have to assault again—but this time against an enemy threatened from flank and rear; and probably ready to retire.

On August 9 we received orders to take over Pope's Post and to hand over Quinn's to the 3rd Regiment. We held Pope's for the next three weeks—during which nothing of particualr interest happened to us, though the fate of the whole campaign was being decided on our left. This will be briefly dealt with later. Each day brought much work and took its toll of casualties. On August 12 we sent 12 snipers to Suvla Bay on special duty. The sick rate was very high, the exhausted men having now no incentive to "crack hardy" any longer.

On August 17 Capt. Tiddy the adjutant was evacuated sick and Lieut. Steele was appointed in his place, Lieut-Col. Stodart was still Post Commander at Quinn's and Major Bourne Acting C.O. of the Regiment.

On August 24 40 unfit men were sent off the Post for a rest and a squadron of the 1st L.H. Regiment took their place. The latter returned to their unit on August 29, when we were reinforced by one officer and 39 other ranks, besides which "A" Squadron and the Machine Gun Section of the 11th L.H. Regiment which had just landed, were attached to us for duty. They were under Major J. Loynes and right glad we were to see them.

On September 2 we were told that the Brigade was to rejoin the New Zealand and Australian Division under General Godley; and that the 2nd Australian Division then just arriving on Gallipoli, was to take over Quinn's, Pope's and Walker's Ridge. We were not sorry to know that we would shortly see the last of those places, though so many of our best had given their lives there, that we had a very real tie to the area. How would those new arrivals get to know the ground as we knew it? How long would they take to learn the habits of the enemy snipers, and the tactics necessary to checkmate them? The 17th Australian Infantry Battalion arriving to take over on September 2 seemed to us terribly raw. Compared to our own worn out men they were like a lot of well-fed jolly school boys. But they soon settled into the job as well as the best.

On September 3 "A" Squadron proceeded to the new position Old No. 3 outpost near Sazli Beit Dere—the Regiment less "A" Squadron was Reserve to 17th Battalion. On 5th the remainder of the Regiment marched to Old No. 3 outpost by short stages—many of the men being unfit for even that effort.

On September 8 Lieut-Col. Stodart was evacuated for a surgical operation and Major Glasgow was appointed to command the Regiment. He was promoted to be Lieut.-Col. a few weeks later.

Our relief from Pope's Hill concluded our front line work on Gallipoli and a brief review of the operations at Sulva Bay and by the New Zealand and Australian Division at Chunuk Bair and Hill 971 etc., are here necessary.

On August 7 the New Zealand Infantry Brigade advanced up Rhododendron Ridge; further North the Indian Brigade attacked Chunuk Bair; while still further north the 4th Australian Infantry Brigade had for its objective that well-known peak, the key of the situation—Hill 971. The difficulties of that night march, over broken and unexplored ground, intersected by innumerable steep ravines which swung the columns out of their bearings, were tremendous. The troops, too, like our own men were weak and ill. The fatigue of the night march exhausted them. In spite of all this, the columns made good progress—but they were forestalled by our mobile enemy, who counter attacked repeatedly and most vigourously. After suffering very severe losses by a withering fire directed from the higher ground, and after most gallant and sustained efforts, our men were compelled to dig in, considerably short of their objectives.

The Divisions at Suvla Bay, instead of seizing "W" Hills and Chocolate Hills at once, appeared to have frozen. They had been landed without maps, information, or guides. The result was that though their objectives had not been held by the enemy on August 7 and 8 and could easily have been occupied then, they wasted precious days and allowed the enemy to fortify the positions. Though this Force was to have been a main factor in the operation, it did did not link up with the left of the New Zealand and Australian Division whose attack on Hill 971 and Chunuk Bair it was supposed to support.

The 1st L.H. Brigade had hoped to act as Advance Guard to this Division; and had that role been assigned to us, there might have been a different story to tell. The failure of this surprise operation settled the fate of the whole Gallipoli expedition, which could not now possibly succeed without very strong reinforcements.

At Old No. 3 outpost we occupied the second line of defence with the attached squadron (11th Regiment.) The remainder of the Regiment was in reserve and was employed in digging sunken roads for mule transport, improving communication trenches etc. The health of the men began to improve—chiefly because they got a full night's sleep for the first time since May 13, and partly because of improved rations. It was now possible occasionally to get a little tinned milk, rice, and on very rare occasions eggs. The bivouac area was shelled frequently and in addition we suffered some casualties while digging.

On September 20 Major Bourne (second in command) was evacuated ill and Capt. Markwell temporarily assumed those duties.

On September 29 reinforcements arrived and on October 2 a further batch of 39 men under Capt Logan and Lt. Evans.

On October 27 we drew timber and iron to build winter quarters. Hitherto such material had been almost impossible to procure—though some enterprising men had managed to "suovenir" or wangle some, by representing themselves to the O/C Engineer's Dump as authorised parties to draw the stores.

The weather was now much colder and the men rather welcomed the daily digging, of which there seemed to be no end. The sniping from a commanding Turkish post known as "Sniper's Nest" was very deadly In addition the bivouac area was shelled periodically. Our issue on November 10 lasted for nearly two hours and caused several casualties. The beach areas too, about this time, were being badly knocked about by shell fire, even the hospitals being repeatedly hit.

On November 10 five officers and 190 other ranks left for Mudros for a rest. Those who had been longest on Gallipoli were selected. Ever since September parties of war worn men had been sent in rotation to Mudros for a fortnight's spell—where they could get undisturbed sleep, some amusement, bathing without the attentions of Beachy Bill, and where rations could be supplemented by canteen stores. The Infantry who had borne the brunt of the fighting were of course the first to be spelled— but now it was our turn. It was like a holiday from school.

The portion of the Regiment remaining on Gallipoli consisted of the

Squadron of the 11th L.H. (attached) and a handful of our old men including the adjutant, Capt. Steele and the signallers. Major Loynes of 11th L.H. was temporarily in charge.

The Anzac position had been inspected on November 13 by no less a person than Lord Kitchener himself and there was much speculation as to the reason for his visit and to its probable result. The idea of a possible evacuation was not entertained by the men.

The daily routine to November 26 consisted of digging and being well shelled. On that day orders were issued for complete silence for 24 hours—no gun or rifle to be fired, or even a bomb thrown. This was extended for a further 24 hours. The idea was apparently to encourage the enemy to expose himself and perhaps attack. On 28th a demonstration was ordered throughout the whole area. A heavy fall of snow occurred on that day—the first that most of us had ever seen. It caused a good deal of discomfort as the men's shelters were very primitive. Our daily routine was not disturbed till December 12. Though we did not know it the fate of the Gallipoli expedition was being debated both by the War Council of the British Cabinet and by the Allied Council in France. Lord Kitchener was in favour of withdrawing from Salonica and employing the troops from there in a final thrust at Anzac or Suvla. The French Government was emphatically opposed to this and was strong enough to prevent the withdrawl from Salonica—the only place from which reinforcements for the Dardenelles could possibly be drawn. Further, our Intelligence Officers had learnt that heavy guns and howitzers were being sent from Germany to the Turks. Though no human force could have driven us from our positions, the guns now spoken of could have blown the narrow and dominated area, and us with it, into the sea. To remain where we were was to court disaster—and on December 7 confidential orders to evacuate Sulva and Anzac were received by the C. in C. These were not passed to units till December 12. The arrangements and orders for the evacuation were worked out in wonderful detail by the Corps Staff. Had the enemy had a hint of what was intended our losses would have been very heavy—estimated by some at 30 per cent. of the whole force. A gradual thinning of the line was carried out from December 12 onwards, by all Brigades.

On December 14 the 2nd Regiment took over Destroyer Hill from the 3rd Regiment which thereupon embarked. On 18th we were reinforced by one man—our C/O Lieut.-Col Glasgow, who had returned from Mudros (some whispered against orders) for the purpose of personally supervising the very responsible work of evacuating that portion of the Regiment which remained on the Peninsula.

To mislead the enemy into considering them normal, periods of "silence" had been kept. Many ingenious devices were rigged up, to fire rifles or bombs, after the troops had left. The mental strain on the last parties to leave was very great. A strong post had been formed which was to have been held by the Rear Party under Colonel Paton, in the event of the enemy discovering how thin the line really was in the final stages, and of his attacking.

Guns and valuable stores were removed nightly. Any unusual movement during daylight was forbidden.

On December 18 at 12 midnight the last 2nd Regiment men (Signallers under Sergt. Peterson) left the trenches, wended their way to the beach, and embarked for Murdos. To December 17 fully 15,000 men had been evacuated and there remained about 20,000 to embark. These were reduced to 10,000 on the morning of 19th. By 10 p.m. on 19th there was only one man to every eight yards of front on the whole position. These were kept busy simulating normality. The last men were withdrawn about 3 a.m. on the morning of 20th. A party of 1st L.H. Regiment holding No. 1 outpost was among the very last to be recalled. At 4 a.m. the evacuation was completed—with a loss of only one man wounded. This wonderful result was achieved by excellent staff work and the intelligent co-operation of all ranks. The first the Turks knew of it was when our mines which had been ready charged days before, were exploded, blowing in their front trenches at some points.

The British position at Cape Helles was evacuated early in January. The 2nd Regiment concentrated at East Mudros on December 19 and embarked on the "Ionian" on 22nd leaving Mudros at midnight. So it happened that we spent the second Christmas of the war, at sea. On 27th we arrived at Alexandria and proceeded straight to our old camp at Heliopolis. How glad we were to see our horses again, and to find so many men of the old originals, who had been wounded, now fit and waiting for us.

CHAPTER V.

UPPER EGYPT

DURING the latter part of 1915 the agents of Germany had contrived to stir up trouble among the warlike Senouissi Arabs of Western Egypt and these constantly threatened the Nile Valley. For the protection of the district a considerable force had been maintained in Upper and Western Egypt and the 1st L.H. Brigade was attached to it. We spent till January 15 reorganising and refitting and on 14th moved to the Barrage and on 16th to Wardan where we were on outpost duty for a fortnight.

Early in February our Commanding Officer Lieut.-Col T. W. Glasgow, D.S.O., was appointed to command the 13th Infantry Brigade. While we rejoiced at his well merited promotion we realised what a loss the Regiment was to sustain. His soldierly qualities had made him most conspicious throughout the Brigade and had earned him the respect and affection of every man in his Regiment. General Glasgow took with him Capt. Steele the adjutant and many promising N.S.Os and men whom we could ill spare. Practically all of them were given Commissions in the Infantry, which arm, owing to the reorganisation, offered rapid promotion.

Major S. W. Barlow of 11th L.H. Regiment was appointed to command the 2nd Regiment with Lieut. Norris as adjutant. The Senior officers with the Regiment at this stage were Major Markwell ("A" Squadron), Major Shanahan ("B" Squadron), and Major Chambers ("C" Squadron). Major Coucher was in charge of details at the Base. Colonel C. F. Cox was now in command of the Brigade vice Major-General Chauvel, promoted to command the newly formed Anzac Mounted Division.

On February 13 we moved to El Minia. On 18th the Regiment was distributed as follows: El Minia—one troop "C" Squadron (under Lieut. Righetti); Nallet-el-Abin, "B" Squadron (under Major Shanahan); Tukh-el-Kheil "C" Squadron, less one troop (Major Chambers); Hassan Pasha "A" Squadron (Major Markwell). Daily patrols were carried out. The weather was wretched—Khamseens being frequent. On March 10 the Regiment went via Roda, Deirut, Manfalut to Assiut a very considerable town on the Nile. Here we left "C" Squadron—the remainder of the Regiment marching on to Sohag, an important administrative centre.

Major Bourne rejoined the Regiment on March 12 and resumed duties of Second in Command.

This expedition was purely protective and was undertaken partly to give confidence to the friendly natives of Upper Egypt and partly to warn the hostile. No enemy were actually encountered by us, but it gave us the opportunity to train the reinforcements in mounted work. We had the misfortune to lose several men by sickness and Private Leatch was drowned in a canal on March 3—having been knocked off a narrow bridge by his horse.

At Easter time 1916 we received news of the disastrous attacks by the

LIEUT.-COL. SYDNEY W. BARLOW
Commanding Officer—February, 1916 to June, 1916

Turks on the posts east of the Canal, at Katia, Duiedar and Hammisah, which had been held by the Warwick, Worcester and Gloucester Yeomanry; and our anticipations that we would be moved there were justified. On May 11 and 13 the Regiment entrained from Assiut and Sohag respectively, for Kantara. On 18th idem we crossed the Canal to Hill 70 and on 26th we marched to Romani, 22 miles from the Canal and about 7 miles from the ancient Pelusium.

SINAI

CHAPTER VI.

THE following were the senior officers of the Regiment at the opening of this campaign:—

Commanding Officer .. .. .. Lieut.-Colonel S. W. Barlow
Second-in-Command .. .. Major G. H. Bourne
O/C "A" Squadron .. .. .. ·· .. Major W. E. Markwell
O/C "B" Squadron .. .. Major M. Shanahan
O/C "C" Squadron .. .. Capt C. C. Stodart
(vice Major Chambers, ill)
O/C Machine-gun Section .. .. Lieut. H. Hackney
Adjutant .. .. Lieut. J. Wasson
Q.M. .. .. Hon. Lieut. F. J. Hockey
M.O. .. .. Capt. Arnold
Chaplain .. .. Capt. H. K. Gordon

Our horses at this time were nearly all suffering from Nile fever, contracted in Upper Egypt, and required nursing. The men, too, had had a severe gruelling with the climate.

At Romani we had relieved the Second Brigade, and it was not long before we were introduced to the wearisome desert patrols that were to try the endurance of both men and horses for months to come. After their successful raid above-mentioned, the Turks had withdrawn across the desert. Their patrols, mounted on camels, were encountered at Bir-el-Abd, Salmana, Bay'ud, etc. Posts in some strength were at Mazar, and El Arish, distant 37 and 56 miles respectively from Romani.

From May 29 to 31 we acted as covering troops to the N.Z.M.R. Brigade who made a reconnaissance of Bir Salmana, 25 miles distant. Water was difficult to obtain, and brackish—boiled, it made most atrocious tea, but passable coffee. It was some time before the horses could be induced to do more than sip it, and their condition suffered accordingly. The weather was very hot, travelling over the heavy sand was most laborious. For ten minutes in each marching hour we dismounted, and led the horses in order to save them as much as possible.

At daylight on June 1 we were visited by our first enemy aeroplane, which dropped six bombs in our very congested Brigade camp area. (Brigade Staffs in those days had not learned to scatter their units). The 3rd Regiment, who were camped next to us, lost many men and horses; and in addition, a large proportion of the horses of the Brigade stampeded. Many, maddened with terror, galloped themselves to death in the desert. We were now taking our turn in a regular roster of long distance patrols— but touch was seldom gained—the wily Turk knowing well that it was no use his trying to repeat his Easter raid, and knowing, too, that we were bent on revenge. Want of water, and the great difficulty of mov-

PLATE 2

SINAI, PALESTINE AND SYRIA

ing supplies over the desert, limited the scope of these patrols to 20 or 25 miles from Romani.

From June 10 to 12 we made a reconnaissance of Bir-Bay'ud, and exchanged shots with enemy patrols. Our horses, however, were not fit to pursue the enemy, who were mounted on camels, as we had the long journey home to look forward to.

Lieut.-Colonel Barlow was evacuated, sick, on June 16, and as Major Bourne was temporarily in charge of 3rd Regiment, Major Markwell assumed command.

Repeated patrols to Oghratina, Hod-el-Ge'Elia, Mushalfat, and Bir-el-Mageibra, etc., occupied the balance of the month. On account of the mishap to the Yeomanry, the higher Command insisted on these patrols being undertaken by whole Regiments or Brigades; and they thus proved most exhausting. We were visited almost daily by hostile 'planes, as at this time the enemy had complete mastery of the air. There was no chance of concealment, so whenever the alarm was given, the horses had to be led off the lines and scattered. Major Bourne returned and assumed command on June 30. July was occupied with long patrols twice a week. The odd days in camp were employed in strengthening the Romani position, as it was reported that the Turks intended to attack us in force and endeavour once more to reach the Canal. A redoubt was ordered to be built on Katib Ganit. Only those who know that mass of ever-shifting sand can appreciate the difficulty of the task. These works too, had to be manned each night; so that men got no rest whatever and were beginning to show it. By the middle of July there was no doubt as to the intentions of the enemy, and he continued to push forward, strengthening tactical positions as he advanced. His skilful use of these in his subsequent withdrawal, we experienced at Katia, Bir-el-Abd, etc. On 20th we had our first brush with him near Oghratina. A patrol in charge of Trooper Gibbs got touch about 9 a.m., and "A" Squadron pushed in and deployed in order to ascertain what the Turks were up to. They came under heavy fire. Trooper Gibbs being wounded, Corporal Cowley and Troopers Nash and Apelt pluckily went to his assistance and got him to safety, but he died in the ambulance cart before reaching the Field Hospital. On July 30 Major Birkbeck resumed duty with the Regiment (after being wounded for the second time on Gallipoli) and took over "A" Squadron. Major Markwell assumed duties of Second-in-Command.

Late in the afternoon of August 1, it became necessary to send rations and water, from Romani, per camel, to the post holding Hill 110, in order to allow them to remain in touch with the enemy there. The Regiment was at Katia, and in contact with the Turks, but Brigade Headquarters ordered an escort to the convoy to be formed from Quarter-masters' offsiders, farriers, and "light duty" men remaining in camp. Corporal Thorn was placed in charge. The instructions he received were of the vaguest, and he had no compass to steer by. Darkness set in before he had gone two miles, and under it's friendly cover, the Turks swung their right flank forward, and as luck would have it, right across Thorn's path. The result was inevitable; the party walked right into the advancing enemey who withheld their fire till the escort had but litle chance of escape and

LIEUT.-COL. G. H. BOURNE, D.S.O., V.D.
Commanding Officer—June, 1916 to April, 1919

no chance of protecting the convoy. Trooper Kennett and Driver Day were taken prisoners. It is with regret that we have to record their deaths while in captivity, within two days of each other. Corporal Thorn and Troopers Patterson and King, making a wide detour, reached camp during the night, and Trooper Jenkins, two days later, after a most exciting experience.

Just before dusk on the afternoon of August 3, the Brigade was ordered out to occupy a line of observation posts from Katib Ganit to Mount Meredith, thence to a point one mile S.E. of Hod Enna. The 3rd Regiment with their left flank resting on the Romani redoubts, held from Katib Ganit to Mount Meredith inclusive (1½ miles). The 2nd Regiment were given from Mount Meredith, exclusive, to the extreme right (2½ miles). The 1st Regiment were in reserve. It was anticipated that the Turks would attack with in a few days, and as the above line of advance was perfectly open, the Brigade was thrown out thus hurriedly in order to give warning. The positions were not entrenched and indeed were not reached in many cases until after dark; but the picquets lost no time in improvising sand "possies," though without sand-bags and revetting material these were not very effective.

The Regiment was disposed as follows:—

"B" Squadron (Major Shanahan), left half of line, keeping touch with 3rd Regiment on their left. "A" Squadron (Major Birkbeck) right half of the line. Two machine-guns under Lieut. Hackney were posted in the centre, covering the main approach from Hod Enna. "C" Squadron in support under Captain C. C. Stodart. The difficulty in keeping touch in this extraordinarily deceptive country, can hardly be exaggerated. The line was a succession of sand dunes, each the counterpart of the other; and in most cases the sides were so steep that detours of up to half a mile were necessary to get round them—and if the next post was only half a mile away by direct line, it was a regular pilgrimage to acutally reach it in the pitch dark. The Squadrons holding the line were less than 100 strong each, so that we had, say, 200 men to about 4,000 yards.

The N.Z.M.R. Brigade had been in touch with the enemy all day at Katia, and they passed back to their camp at Et Maler, through our line, about 2030 (8.30 p.m.) Their rear-guard passed through about 2115 (9.15 p.m.) Apparently the Turks followed close on their heels, for at 2150 the first shots were exchanged between an "A" Squadron picquet and the enemy advance guard, near Hod Enna. This was immediately reported to Brigade Headquarters, and to 3rd Regiment. In a few minutes, our line was being probed from end to end. As it was now obvious that the threatened attack had come, and that the collision was not a mere matter of patrols, it became necessary to thicken and shorten the line, which was in imminent danger of being broken through at any minute. One troop of "C" Squadron, under Lieut. Righetti, to which was attached some details of Regimental Staff, was sent to fill the gap between the right of "B" Squadron and the left of the Machine-gun position. Urgent orders were also sent to Major Birkbeck to withdraw his Squadron, and the machine-guns from the right of the line, and to take up a position in rear of the Regiment's left. This was a matter of considerable difficulty in the dark, owing to the nature of the ground. About 0100 in the morning of 4th, "B" Squadron reported that they were being attacked in strength. A similar report was received from 3rd Regiment. Additional s.a. ammunition was sent to "B" Squadron and they were told to hold on at all costs; as had the enemy broken through there, the whole of the right of the line would have been cut off. The pressure by the enemy now increased. This was reported to Brigade Headquarters, and immediately afterwards the telephone line was cut. We had no further communication with Brigade Staff, nor inded saw any of them till noon next day. Acting on the last message they received from us, however, a Squadron of 1st Regiment was sent in support, but it did not arrive till after 0330. About 0200 the balance of "C" Squadron was put in to line; in spite of which the enemy pressure was such that it was obvious we could not hold him much longer. At 0240, no Officer being available for the duty, a N.C.O. was sent back to select a position to retire to. The enemy at this time seemed to be making his main attack on Mount Meredith; and the 3rd Regiment there and our "B" Squadron were having very lively fighting. At the same time the enemy's main column was marching from Hod Enna past our shortened right flank towards Mount Royston. Anxiously we waited for word from Major Birkbeck as to whether he had succeeded in withdrawing, and just as anxiously we waited for the first streaks of dawn, for there was no question that the darkness was our best ally, and that in daylight we must be overwhelmed. About 0300, the enemy captured Mount Meredith and the 3rd Regiment was forced to withdraw its's right, thus exposing our left. No word had been received from Major Birkbeck, and it was yet too soon to assume that he had completed his march in rear of us, to his new position. Major Markwell had been sent to direct and hasten that operation, but had had difficulty in finding him owing to the darkness. In order to give his party time to reach safety, we therefore held on. At this juncture Lieut. Righetti was killed, and several men were hit. At 0320, being surrounded on three sides and the firing line having been forced back to the led horses, the order was given to withdraw to the position already selected.

The Turks were now in many cases only 50 yards off, and several amusing incidents occurred. One man who had secured his horse offered to take a dismounted man doubleback, and found the other chap was a Turk. Several horses were killed, and the barefooted enemy being quicker over the sand than our boys, who were handicapped with boots and leggings, took several prisoners.

Which of us will forget the scamper away? How so many did get away is a marvel. The bullets were making little spurts of flame all round and among us, on striking the sand. Here we experienced for the first time, the moral effect of turning our backs on the enemy, and the question arose in our minds as we rode, "Can we reform?" The order "Sections about— Action front" was given as we reached the position, and was splendidly carried out. This high test of discipline gave us renewed confidence in ourselves. Here too- we were joined by the Squadron of 1st Regiment which had been sent out to our support. The ridge was held till daylight, when to our great relief, Major Birkbeck's party could be seen laboriously making it's way through the heavy sand, on our right. From here, back to Et Mala near the main Romani position, each ridge in succession was held, till the enemy, ever working round our right, outflanked and enfiladed us or our horses. Each time we withdrew, we looked for signs of some support. We expected a Brigade of Infantry to be taking up a position in our rear, or at least that our guns would support us from Romani. About 0500, Lieut. Woodyatt was killed, and shortly afterwards Major Shanahan was wounded. A number of other ranks had become casualties, but all things considered, we got off very lightly. And now, at about 0600, we could see the 2nd Brigade coming out to support us. The enemy pressure, too, slackened off a little, as their main force continued to march towards Mount Royston, and across our front, thus threatening the railway, south east of Romani. The line by this time was decidedly mixed, as we had been joined by one Squadron of 1st Regiment, and part of 3rd Regiment. When the 2nd Brigade arrived, that part of 1st Brigade remaining was withdrawn from the line to reform, and for the rest of the morning, was held as Divisional Reserve; C.O., 2nd Regiment having reported to General Chauvel about 0800.

At noon the Regiment was placed under Brig.-General Royston of 2nd Brigade—the 6th Regiment temporarily coming to 1st Brigade. General Royston was the man of the hour, and seemed to thoroughly enjoy the situation. We took it as a great compliment to be placed under his command. We had ample troops (but to this moment, only part of Anzac Division had been employed, together with a couple of batteries) and now that the intention of the enemy, and his objective had been disclosed, it was a simple matter to check him. The Turks, too, were showing signs of fatigue, having made a rapid night march, and been hung up quite unexpectedly by the 1st Brigade improvised outpost. We had the satisfaction of knowing that our strenuous night's fighting, by forcing the enemy to deploy before he intended, upset his plans and was a big factor in the subsequent victory. Through our temporary transfer to 2nd Brigade we came in for the outpost on the night of the 4th also. We prolonged the right of the 7th Regiment towards Mount Royston, and before dawn on 5th, both Regiments in a long, and very thin, line advanced with the bayonet towards Mount Meredith, sweeping all the Turks off Wellington Ridge, on which they had their main force. The 2nd Brigade on that day consisted of the 2nd and 7th L.H. Regiments and the Wellington Mounted Rifles. The 5th L.H. Regiment was holding Duiedar about 8 miles south east.

Our Regiment thus had the honour of "Opening the Ball" in the Sinai-Palestine-Syria Campaign; and did so in a most creditable manner.

The bulk of the Turkish force made their escape to Katia, but we got nearly 1,000 prisoners, some machine-guns, etc. Our led horses were now brought up and all mounted troops started to Katia in pursuit. Our horses were too exhausted to permit of a wide flanking movement of the Katia position, and the frontal attack was unable to make any impression on the enemy.

"A" Squadron was detailed to keep touch between the N.Z.M.R. Brigade and the 3rd L.H. Brigade and came under heavy shell fire   The remainder of the Regiment was in reserve on this day (August 5).

On the afternoon of 5th we were retransferred to 1st L.H. Brigade.

As our horses had now been without water for 52 hours, and the men without rations for a day, we were withdrawn to Romani to rest. The men were quite exhausted after two nights in succession without sleep; and the weather was very hot.

The following casualties had been suffered by the Regiment:

Killed: Two officers and seven other ranks.

Died of Wounds: One other rank.

Wounded: Two officers and twenty other ranks.

Taken Prisoners: Eight other ranks.

Troopers McColl, Hobson, Littler and Handsley survived their captivity, and were repatriated; but is with deep regret that we have to record the deaths of Sergt. Drysdale, Corporals Somerville and Easton and Trooper Ward while in the hands of the Turk.

On 6th, we buried dead and collected enemy material that had been abandoned. The higher command ruled that we were not fit to pursue owing to exhaustion of men and horses.

On 8th, we marched out with the object of again attacking the enemy's rear guard at Bir-el-Abd, distant 22 miles. The position was reached at daylight on 9th. A hot engagement was fought, but the Turks were too well prepared for us, and we were obliged to return, for rations and water, nearer our base, viz.—Oghratina. In this engagement the Regimental casualties were:— Killed, one; wounded, ten.

We again had a very warm corner in this action and covered the withdrawal when that, unfortunately, became necessary.

This was the last attempt to molest the Turkish retreat. Had full use been made of our mobility at the outset, not a Turk or a gun would have got away.

On 13th we returned to Romani and were congratulated, and thanked by the Brigadier, Colonel Meredith, for the work we had done. The health of the men had been greatly impaired by the arduous desert patrolling, and night work from May to date, and it was necessary to nurse them and the horses. Work was accordingly slackened off till the middle of September, when it was rumoured that we were to be armed for shock tactics. Sword exercise was ordered for Officers in addition to the ordinary training programme. Lectures were given each evening on military subjects.

Honours awarded for services in the field to date are quoted in the Appendix.

Our signallers were about this time re-organised under a Signalling Officer, Lieut. Letch (formerly of 1st L.H. Brigade Signallers); and their efficiency improved greatly.

On September 30 we moved to Kantara for six weeks spell, during which, officers were sent to the Cavalry School, and men went on leave to Alexandria and Port Said, in batches of twenty.

This break was very welcome to both men and horses. For those who did not experience it, it is difficult to realise how thoroughly exhausted we were after this first strenuous summer in the desert. Of relief, by way of leave, there had been none. Water was scarce and very often brackish.

Though the Y.M.C.A. had been with us from the start, they had great difficulties to overcome in the way of transport, as the Railway did not reach Romani till July. A.I.F. Canteens had not got into their stride, and there were no means of varying the rations. In addition, the tactical work had been a severe strain; and is by no means represented by the number of engagements fought.

On November 15 our spell being over, we marched via Duiedar and Romani to Ge'Eila, a large Hod about 5 miles east of Bir el Abd—forming with the Anzac Mounted Division (less second Brigade), part of "Desert Column" under Major-General Sir P. Chetwode, Bart. The railway, by this, had been pushed to Bir el Abd and Salmana; and thanks to the good work of the E.L.C. (Egyptian Labour Corps) it was being laid at the rate of a mile per diem. The enemy was in strength at Mazar, 12 miles distant, and Desert Column was being assembled as rapidly as supplies and transport permitted, with the object of attacking him there.

Simultaneously with the railway, a freshwater main was being laid, which carried filtered Nile water all the way from the sweet-water canal at Kantara. This main was continued as far, ultimately, as Belah and We'l: Sheikh Nuran, and watered up to 100,000 men and 30,000 horses. From "Pipehead," the water was distributed by means of 12 gallon tanks ("fanatis") two of which were carried on a camel. The railway and water main were two of the chief factors in the success of the campaign.

At the time of which we are writing, protection of the Column devolved chiefly on the 1st L.H. Brigade, so that we came in for our full share of patrols, outposts, etc.

From Hod el Ge'Eila we moved northwards to Arnussi and then to Gererat which was within striking distrance of Mazar. A very welcome Christmas mail was received here, including parcels and a large consignment of "X'mas Billies" from our Regimental Comforts Fund Committee in Brisbane. Every man received at least one parcel—but as an early move with the minimum transport was imminent, the contents could not be held over for the festive season, and were consumed in advance.

Before a blow could be considered, however, it was necessary to have definite information as to the prospects of getting water in the enemy territory. Captain W J. Brown was selected to take a party of 20 men, with three engineers and a spear-head boring plant, to prospect for water in the Wadi el Arish, well behind the enemy's lines. For communications he took a Helio and a basket of carrier pigeons. The point to be reached was 30 miles distant, the country very rough indeed, occupied by hostile Bedouins who were bound to give information of the exped'tion to the enemy, even if patrols were avoided. But the chief difficulty was, that if no water was found, the party would have nothing to drink till it returned to camp. This actually proved to be the case. The party reached its objective, put down three bores without success, gained valuable information about the country, avoided enemy patrols and regained camp after an absence of 30 hours; both horses and men being exhausted by the difficult march and want of water.

A similar patrol was sent out by the 1st Regiment two days later but it had no better luck. Information having reached the Turks that these two patrols had penetrated their lines, however, they became nervous as to the safety of Mazar. They therefore evacuated that place and concentrated their force at El Arish. The instant this became known to General Chetwode, he ordered the advance on El Arish. This was accomplished by the Anzac Division (less 2nd Brigade) and Camel Corps marching round it during the night—the Infantry of the Column moving on the place by direct road. By daylight it was surrounded; but the birds had flown. Having found that our horses were equal to such performances as that of Captain Brown's patrol, the Turks knew they were not safe at El Arish, and consequently sought the security of Magdhaba, evacuating the former place just before our arrival. Magdhaba was distant 27 miles, along a practically unknown and waterless track, but in spite of that, and the fact that the Column had just had one night march General Chetwode decided to surprise the Turks there at dawn on December 23 with the mounted troops of his command, viz:— 1st. 3rd and N. Z. M. R. Brigades, and Imperial Camel Corps, 18th Brigade, R. H. A. and Hong Kong and Singapore Mountain Battery.

After a long and tiresome wait for rations to come up we accordingly started on the night of December 22 for Magdhaba—"C" Squadron, 2nd Regiment being Advance Guard. The enemy position was very difficult to locate; his trenches were beautifully sited. The attack was opened by the Camel Brigade. The 1st Brigade went in on their right—the 3rd Brigade and N.Z.M.R. Brigade on their left, practically enveloping the position. The situation was, that the Turks were sitting on the only water within miles; and the position had either to be taken or we would go thirsty for at least 24 hours

The Turk has ever proved himself a splendid and stubborn fighter from behind cover. So, in this case we found the job much more difficult than had been anticipated. This Regiment was not engaged as a unit; having been detailed as Brigade Reserve and split up in different jobs. The final result however, was largely contributed to by the energy of Major Markwell, who gathered up some details of 3rd Regiment in addition to three troops of "B" Squadron, 2nd Regiment under Major Chambers, and successfully led them against the chief remaining enemy redoubt. Major Birkbeck skilfully led two troops right round the position and threatened a mounted attack from the enemy's only line of retreat. This manoeuvre decided the Turkish Commander to hoist the white flag; the entire force surrendering.

Lieutenant Guiren, of this Regiment, and his troop, just beat the 3rd Brigade into Magdhaba itself.

The enemy force of about 2500 was captured or killed. We also got a battery of Mountain guns, about 2,000 rifles; machine guns, s.a.a. etc., and many horses and mules.

The 1st Regiment was detailed to clear up the battlefield, and bivouaced for the night; and 2nd Regiment was detailed to escort the prisoners to El Arish—another night march thus being necessary. During the previous 84 hours we had practically no sleep, so that the journey back was by no

MAJOR W. E. MARKWELL, D.S.O.
Commanding temporarily—January to February, 1916

means a pleasant one; men went fast asleep on their horses or camels, some falling off. Most of us experienced optical delusions, induced by want of sleep. We halted to ration at Lafan, half-way to El Arish. Our bivouacs at El Arish were reached at dawn on Christmas Eve The weather was wet and of course there were no tents owing to want of transport—indeed it was proving a difficult matter to even feed us as we had got so far beyond Railhead—the trackless sand rendering wheeled vehicles of little use. Much heavy work was therefore thrown on the excellent Camel Transport Corps.

The prisoners were handed over by Major Stodart before noon on 24th. In order to ration them, our friends of 52nd Division had to go short for a day or two. The "Scotties" were amusingly indignant, and repeatedly told our fellows they had taken too —— many prisoners, and should have used the —— bayonet more.

Christmas was hardly a "cheerful" day. When the rain and duties permitted we spent the time trying to make up some back sleep which was urgently required. Everybody attempted something in the nature of X'mas dinner of course, though there was little but rations to do it on and it had to be consumed standing up, holding food or mug at arms length, to avoid the cataract from one's hat.

The enemy held two very strong posts near Rafa and Weli Sheikh Nuran, and these required our next attention—being distant from El Arish, 21 and 28 miles respectively. Accordingly a reconnaissance of the former was made by the 1st L.H. Brigade on December 30. We arrived at Sheikh Zowaiid before dusk and just in time to allow Brig-General Cox and his escort to ride towards Magruntein and carry out the reconnaissance. The main enemy position was found to be on this latter place, and about 2½ miles S.W. of Rafa. The garrison was estimated at about 1,000. We camped for a few hours at Sheikh Zowaiid (one of the coldest nights we experienced) and started back to El Arish before daylight. The enemy's patrols had apparently not observed us; but of course they soon heard all about us from the Bedouins, who had done a thriving trade with us in fowls and eggs during our halt.

Orders to attack Magruntein were prepared immediately the reconnaissance report was received; and, as at Magdhaba, the mounted troops of Desert Column, strengthened by the addition of 5th Cavalry Brigade (Yeomanry), were detailed for the duty. The following artillery was attached—Inverness and Ayrshire Batteries, R.H.A., Somersets and H.A.C., with Hong-Kong and Singapore Mountain Battery. The whole was under command of Major-General Sir P. Chetwode—Major-General Sir Harry Chauval being in charge of Anzac Division.

The above Column moved from El Arish at 1700 on January 8, 1917. An all night march enabled us to surround the position from south and east, considerably before daylight, and then occurred an unavoidable delay, owing to the necessity of rounding up hostile Bedouins.

The N.Z.M.R. Brigade had furtherest to go, and accompanied by a political officer, they were instructed to search the Police Post and huts at Rafa for documents, before advancing on Magruntein from north west. The 1st Brigade attacked from north and were first in action—the Camel

Brigade attacked from the east and the Yeomanry from the south. The 3rd Brigade (less 8th Regiment) was ultimately sent in between 1st Brigade and the Camels. The 8th Regiment was sent to keep the enemy force at We'Li Sheikh Nuran under observation and to intercept probable reinforcements. The 1st and 2nd Regiments were sent in first—3rd Regiment being Brigade reserve. It was now after 0900 and the enemy had a magnificent field of fire. We were fortunate in being able to reach a road, running parallel with our advancing line, and which was sunken in a few places, thus affording the only available cover; from where we attempted places, thus affording the only available cover. From there we attempted to develop superiority of fire, waiting till our guns could knock out the particularly well posted and his fire very accurate. The distance the N.Z.M.R. Brigade had to cover had been underestimated and it seemed a long while before they got up on our right. The Camel Corps were getting a rough time like ourselves, and the Yeomanry had been forced to withdraw. There was no weight in our attack anywhere, and lack of co-ordination resulted in wasted efforts by individual units. No progress had been made at 1700. A Turkish force was then reported to be advancing from the north and a Regiment was detailed to intercept and engage it.

The situation appeared so critical that General Chetwode ordered withdrawal, believing he had been defeated. The order reached us through Division and Brigade Headquarters. Had it been obeyed, we would have had to abandon some of our wounded. By the greatest good fortune, however, this was prevented. The N.Z. Brigade had not then received the order and continued to press on, and a few Turks fearing the bayonet in the dusk, surrendered This was the signal for us to press on too, and the information that we were advancing and with good prospects, was immediately communicated by the C.O. to the Brigade Major, and by him to Divisional Headquarters. The order to withdraw was therefore cancelled and a general advance ordered, with complete success. The 2nd Regiment telephone was the only one in the line that was working, thanks to the energy of Lieutenant Letch, our Signalling officer, and of Signaller Mercer who had kept it repaired under fire during the day. This enabled the essential information to be transmitted to Divisional H.Q. The guns having ceased fire, the enemy relieving force knew that Magruntein had fallen. They therefore withdrew. The task of removing the wounded and clearing up the field was a long one. The 8th Regiment was detailed as rear party; the remainder leaving at midnight for Sheikh Zowaiid, where we had a couple of hours sleep.

Many of us held the opinion that the position could have been galloped in the dark before the Turks were aware of our presence; and probably with far fewer casualties than we suffered.

The enemy had been taken too cheaply. It was thought that the appearance of horsemen right round him would bluff him into surrendering. (It was time we knew "Jacko" better than that). The result was we had no strength to press an attack anywhere in daylight. In the dark a bayonet advance against Magruntein would have settled the matter in 15 minutes.

Had we pulled out, the moral effect would have been serious.

The Column and Divisional Commanders had the Brigade paraded when we got back to El Arish and thanked us for our work at Magdhaba and

Rafa. For services rendered, especially in those two battles, two officers were awarded D.S.O.'s (See appendix.)

The Regiment suffered the following casualties:—

Killed: Eight other ranks.

Died of Wounds: Three other ranks.

Wounded: Eight other ranks.

While in bivouac at El Airsh we were subjected to a good deal of bombing day and night; and the "returned empties" of our very feeble anti-aircraft artillery were perhaps as trying to the nerves as the bombs.

Lieut.-Colonel G. H. Bourne was evacuated sick on January 13 and Major W. E. Markwell, D.S.O. assumed command for six weeks, with temporary rank of Lieut.-Col.

The complete success of Magdhaba and Rafa convinced the Turks that detached posts, however strong, were not safe from our active Mounted troops. They therefore withdrew early in February from We'Li Sheikh Nuran and Shellal, to the very strong Gaza—Beersheba line which was to prove such a formidable obstacle and was destined to hold us up till November.

The 2nd. Brigade had been doing Line of Communication work during the past three months, and though we were in need of a spell, we were by no means pleased when the order came for us to exchange places with them. We accordingly moved back to Mazar. "A" Squadron being detached to Malha, and "C" to Gererat.

Musketry and the usual training was carried out here. We also had the precious water pipe line to patrol. On one occasion (not while we were on guard) a hostile airman had daringly landed behind our lines and blown the water main up—a by no means difficult thing to do. It was soon repaired.

Early in March we were moved to Hill 200, near El Arish, holding posts along the wadi to Lahfan, and patrolling to Magdhaba, to protect the right rear of our main force which was just about to attack Gaza. About this time, the 4th Brigade, having been reformed under Brig.-General Meredith, was moving up from the Canal. This necessitated a re-organisation of the mounted troops—we lost our old friends of 3rd Brigade who had hitherto been in Anzac Division, and who were now transferred with the 4th L.H. Brigade to the Australian Division. This reduced the Anzac Division to the normal establishment of three Brigades.

The first battle of Gaza was fought on March 26, 1917. It was a victory turned into defeat by want of nerve. As the Regiment took no part in it, we will not go into details here.

On April 6, we were relieved by the 4th Brigade who had just arrived from the Canal. We then marched to Khan Yunis, where the Column was assembling for the second attack on Gaza. This brought us well into Palestine, to which a new chapter must be devoted.

CHAPTER VII.

PALESTINE

THE Regiment reached Khan Yunis, the point of assembly for the mounted troops for the Second battle of Gaza, on April 8, and camped on the edge of the sand dunes. We drew up to establishment of picks and shovels, with carriers for pack saddles here. Hitherto, picks had not been required, but we were now getting into harder country. Experiments, too, were carried out in packing the recently issued Hotchkiss Automatic Rifle and ammunition, as that laid down was found to be capable of considerable improvement. It was expected that gas would be employed freely in the fighting about to take place. The Divisional Gas Officer and his staff therefore, were kept busy instructing and giving lectures. On April 12, we took over the outpost line, towards Abasan-el-Kebir, from the Warwickshire Yeomanry. We were relieved by the Dorsets on 14th. At 2030 on April 16 we marched out with Anzac Division to Shellal, on Wadi Ghuzze, where we watered at 1030 on 17th. That night we held the outpost line from El Nagili—El Dammath—El Imara—Goz-el-Gelieb; a distance of five miles, so that little more than observation posts could be furnished. We spent a quiet night though there were a few enemy patrols about, one of which was driven off with loss, by a post of "C" Squadron. The Yeomanry relieved us at 0630 on 18th. We rested at Shellal until 2000 that night, when we marched with the Brigade to Khirbet Erk, a point 1½ miles south west of Baiket-el-Sana, a commanding ridge just north of Wadi Imleh, and which was about one mile south west of the Turkish line. We arrived before daylight on 19th. The 1st Regiment had formed the advance guard, and were pushed forward on to the ridge in the early dawn—the 2nd and 3rd Regiments being held in hand, as a break through was expected. The Second battle of Gaza was now proceeding, from the coast, to Tel-el-Sheria and Hareira, a front of 22 miles. The whole of the mounted troops had been thrown in dismounted on the right flank. On our immediate left was the N.Z.M.R. Brigade, and on our right the 2nd Brigade. At 1300 the 2nd Regiment was ordered to relieve the 1st Regiment on Baiket-el-Sana; the 3rd Regiment were ordered to prolong our right and connect up with 2nd Brigade. At this stage it looked as if our role would be a bayonet attack about dusk. The 1st Regiment had had little opposition up to the time of their relief. We trotted up under shell fire, sent our horses back, and commenced to take over just as the Turks advanced against the position. Major Chambers was wounded while laying out trenches for his Squadron to dig. He was dressed by Capt. Machin (Regimental Medical Officer) but died at the Field Hospital, Tel-el-Jemmi. In him we lost a gallant and deservedly popular officer.

The 3rd Regiment (for reasons which will be stated shortly) were not in position on our right. Under the circumstances, the C.O. detained Major

42

A GROUP OF OFFICERS WITH THE REGIMENT—MAY, 1918

Standing: Capt. W. J. Handley, Capt. F. Trinca, M.C. (M.O.) Major J. W. Brown, D.S.O., Major G. Birkbeck, D.S.O., Lt.-Col. G. H. Bourne, D.S.O., Major C. C. Stodart, M.C., Lt. L. B. Guiren, M.C., Lt. H. E. S. Newton, Lt. H. A. Weller.

Middle: Lt. J. M. Wills M.M., (Sigs), Lt. W. K. Thompson, Lt. L. J. Henderson, M.C., Lt. W. J. D. Anderson, Lt. H. P. Mc-Intyre, Lt. A. F. Jones, Lt. W. S. Joyner, Lt. G. W. McIntyre.

Front: Lt. W. K. King, M.C., Lt. G. S. Mackrell, Lt. E. D. Brown, Lt. R. G. Sinton, Lt. G. T. Pledger, M.C., (Adjutant) Capt. F. Evans, M.C.

Smith's Squadron of 1st Regiment till some definite information of the 3rd Regiment could be obtained. It appears that, as the South Australians were moving up, they found the 2nd Brigade were echeloned on our right rear, about two miles away, and that a Brigade of enemy cavalry were assembled, out of sight from us and on our immediate right. The enemy's guns were shelling our led horses, and the Wadi Imleh—His Infantry were pressing us on Sana. His cavalry then seriously threatened our led horses and our rear. The C.O. 3rd Regiment wisely decided to halt under cover and watch the cavalry, advising B.H.Q., of his action and the reason for it. Had he dismounted, his right flank and led horses, as well as ours would have been exposed and would have offered an ideal objective for the enemy's mounted troops. Aggressive action by them would have had very serious consequnces for us; though they would have had to pay dearly for any success. We repulsed the Infantry attack on Sana (our new Hotchkiss Automatic Rifles doing fine work), and held on comfortably; but things were not going well on our left.

In broad daylight, and without knowledge of the C.O. a Staff Officer sent up our led horses, right into the firing line. They, of course, drew considerable shell fire and suffered casualties. The C.O. ordered them back at once, as no word of an intended withdrawal had been received. Word was sent to B.H.Q., that we were able to hold on, with the assistance of one Squadron of 1st Regiment, abovenamed. The unwelcome order to withdraw was received a little later, however, and the led horses were sent up in the dark, this time under Regimental arrangements. The position was evacuated without trouble, and in good order; having been held by us for seven hours. We joined up with Brigade at midnight, and retired to a point half a mile north west of We'Li Sheikh Nuran, arriving there at 1000 on 20th. Our casualties were:—

Killed: One officer and one other rank.
Wounded: Six other ranks.

As the Column moved off, about mid-day, it was heavily bombed by three enemy 'planes. We suffered the following casualties.—

Killed: One officer and one other rank.
Wounded: Seven other ranks.
We also lost forty-one horses.

On the night of April 20, we held an outpost line east of Wadi Ghuzze, near Hisseia. At daylight on 21st, "A" Squadron, under Capt. Handley, got touch with a Regiment of enemy cavalry near Goz-el-Geleib. On evening of 21st, we moved to Abasan-el-Kebir; we were bombed there on 22nd, No. 1096. Tpr. Jarman, E.G., being slightly wounded. On 22nd we moved to Abu Sitta, where we experienced a severe heat wave, made more trying owing to scarcity of water. We were given the duty of putting Hill 310, just north of Hiseia, in state of defence; and made a good job of it in record time in spite of the weather. This was to be a strong post in the new line we were taking up; and which, as far as the mounted troops were concerned, ran from Hill 310 along Wadi Ghuzze, south of Gamli, thence west to Ghabi. The Infantry held the north or left of the line, which was dug a good deal closer to the enemy. On April 27, we again crossed to east of Wadi Ghuzze, and took up the Shellal—Hiseia sector of the line, which we proceeded to dig and wire. Captain R. N. Franklin resumed duty with Regiment on May 6, and took over "A" Squadron. "B" Squadron on death of Major Chambers, came under Captain W. J. Brown. The month of May was devoted to usual outpost duties and patrols, and improving our line.

On May 18, a patrol of two troops, "A" Squadron, under Lieut Mackrell, reached Sausage Ridge, right up against the Turkish line. They drew heavy fire, No. 780. Cpl. T. E. Langridge being killed. Corporal Geddes made a gallant attempt to get him in, but the fire was too hot and he was unable to move him.

On May 22, the Brigade was ordered to act as covering troops to the demolition party who were to blow up the old Turkish railway line, Beersheba towards Auja (near Magdhaba). While this line was in existence our right flank was threatened. Also, even if the Turks had no aggressive intentions in that direction, it suited us to destroy the rails, so that they could not be used elsewhere. For this operation, Beersheba had to be screened in order to prevent any interference with our communications and this duty was entrusted to N.Z.M.R. and 2nd Light Horse Brigades. The Engineers demolition parties with their covering troops had a night march of 32 miles to reach their tasks. The objective was reached just at daylight. The sector allotted to us was Hadaj to Wadi Inkharuba. The operation was completely successful. The demolition was completed by mid-day and we withdrew at once. We reached our bivouac at 2320 (11.30 p.m.) having covered 64 miles in 31 hours.

The Regiment was very weak by this time, and even the arrival of Lieut. Brett and 38 other ranks on May 25, left us far below strength. The end of May saw us spelling for a few days at Kazar, where we went through a musketry course, and whence, being within reasonable distance of the beach, we were able to indulge in the luxury of swimming parades.

On June 19 the whole Brigade was moved to Marakeb (on the beach near Khan Yunis) for a spell. We had a very fine ten days holiday, and plenty of rest—no broken nights—swimming and sports. This will be a place of happy memories for all who were there (in spite of the many inspections, etc.) A couple of Pierrot troupes (one organised from the 1st Brigade by Major Franklin, and one by a Yeomanry Brigade) and a boxing tournament helped to enliven our evenings and carried our thoughts far away from the war. Preparations for two good sports meetings (at which by the way Private Scouller of our "B" Squadron put up the remarkable performance of winning the 100 yards championship, the 220, 440, and 880 yards, high jump, long jump and hurdle races) kept us interested.

On 29th we left Marakeb for Fukhari, en route for Gamli and Ghabi, the most southerly sector of the line. On July 3, the Brigade was ordered to cover a reconnaissance by General Chetwode of portion of the enemy line near Irgeig, and to afford protection to a party of surveyors. We left bivouac at 0100 on 4th and moved to Wadi Hanafish. Touch was gained with the enemy at Hill 550 before dawn, and at Wadi Sufi at 0700. This Regiment pushed on and made sector Hill 730—770, both inclusive. (Near Hareira in the Gaza—Beersheba line.) We were shelled all day with but little effect. The enemy positions and railway line having been plotted on the map by the Engineers, and the reconnaissance, and survey of the area completed, we withdrew at 1800. During the day, the enemy had moved up a couple of additional batteries, and put up a good barrage for us to go through.

This regiment was rear-guard. Thanks to "shell-formation" which we immediately adopted, and to admirable "jinking," we got through with only five men slightly wounded, and formed up out of range without an absentee. The casualties were:—

Wounded: Five other ranks.

This operation demonstrated again the fact that mounted troops, on reasonable ground, can generally avoid heavy losses from artillery, by manoeuvre. The enemy would probably have done better had he used more sharpnel, and less H.E.

We reached Gamli again at 2100. The next fortnight was taken up with patrols in various parts of "No Man's Land" over the whole of which, we had "grazing rights." "Trespassers," in the shape of Turkish patrols, seldom ventured out except under cover of darkness. Our best energies were devoted to catching these patrols. On 18th, it was again our turn for a "Jacko Patrol Drive." Avoiding the Karm road (which was becoming too frequently used) we went to Goz Lakhleilat, about four miles south of Karm, and formed a line about 3 miles long north east and south west to begin the drive, in conjunction with the 3rd Regiment, who were co-operating from further south. When day broke, we found two regiments of Turkish cavalry and a battery at Karm; and very much nearer our lines than we were. The order was immediately passed for the Regiment to concentrate, as in our extended formation, we could have done nothing against the force of enemy, which, happily, was so far ignorant of our presence. Their flanking patrols were however, not long in making themselves a nuisance and forcing us to disclose ourselves; the area we were spread over evidently misleading them as to our strength. Several parties of our fellows had exciting pursuits; those under Sergt. Carlyon, and Lance-Corporal Blacket capturing eleven Lancers. These N.C.O.'s were awarded the "Military Medal" for their initiative and dash. The enemy were thus warned of our presence before we could reform the Regiment; and there was not yet sufficint sun to heliograph the position to Headquarters at camp. The Signallers got the message through a little later, however, and Divisional Headquarters advised that they were sending the 2nd Brigade to our assistance. The C.O. replied: "Unlikely to require assistance 2nd Brigade" and later on when the enemy commenced to withdraw, and our scattered Regiment to concentrate: "Situation well in hand." In spite of these, Corps Headquarters turned out the whole of Anzac and Australian Divisions, who of course only arrived when it was all over. We thought at the time, that the enemy had set a trap for us, but that was only a secondary object; and was not achieved. It was months afterwards that we found that, under cover of that force, German and Turkish Generals had made a reconaissance of our position with the object of attacking us. What a pity they did not do so; our ultimate task would have been much easier.

The following fortnight was taken up in patrols daily (or rather nightly), in order to keep the enemy out of the huge triangle formed "No Man's Land," Gaza being the apex and Beersheba the end of the Turk's side, and Gamli—28 miles east—the end of our side.

On August 2, we laid a telephone cable underground as far as Karm, in anticipation of pending operations. In addition we had several long patrols south of Beersheba, to reconnoitre the locality in which we were to operate in the forthcoming and decisive Third battle of Gaza. On one occasion we furnished protection for a reconnaissance of Beersheba by the new C. in C., General Sir Edmund Allenby, and two of the Corps Commanders, Sir Harry Chauvel and Sir Phillip Chetwode, when, one may presume, the plan for the great battle was being prepared.

Demonstrations by aeroplane contact patrols were given about this time to instruct us in the new and useful method of sending messages and keeping touch during an engagement. Briefly, it was as follows: each troop carried a number of ground flares, and when one of our 'planes came over, flying a pre-arranged signal for purpose of identification, the flares were lit to show the pilot where our front line was. Regimental Headquarters was furnished with large ground sheets, by which they signalled to the pilot, who replied by Klaxon Horn, using morse code.

The collapse of the Russians had enabled the Turks to reinforce the Gaza front very considerably, though opinion was divided between the German and Turkish Generals, as to whether the whole of their forces thus freed should be employed in the Palestine Area or partly in counter-attacking in Mesopotamia.

Plan of the Third Battle of Gaza was roughly as follows: 20th Corps was to attack Beersheba from the south and west, and the enemy line as far north of Beersheba as Irgeig. Desert Mounted Corps was to march via Khalasa and Asluj, and attack Beersheba from east and north east. Beersheba having fallen, 20th Corps was to roll up the line from the south while 21st Corps attacked Gaza, and Desert Mounted Corps simultaneously swept up in rear of the Turkish lines cutting off communications, supplies and reinforcements, and, it was hoped gathering up many prisoners. There was a feeling of cheery confidence throughout the force, inspired undoubtedly, by our new C. in C. For the first time, we were to be really used as mounted troops and to play the part for which we had been trained. Further, the role assigned to us promised opportunities of pursuit and of making victory decisive. The arrangements for transport, supplies, etc., had been extraordinarily well made.

On October 24, we started to move by stages to the position of assembly, which for us, was Asluj. On 27th we reached Esani. From here a Squadron under Capt. W. J. Handley, was sent to Hill 840, six miles west of Beersheba, with orders to entrench and hold it at all costs, in order to deny observation to the enemy. The remainder of the Regiment, was inlying regiment pending this operation. At dawn, Capt. Handley was relieved by a Squadron of 3rd Regiment, and "C" Squadron of 2nd Regiment moved out to support them. We reached Asluj on night of October 29. Large parties had, of course, been at work improving the wells there and in building storage tanks, but even so, "Q" Branch had great difficulty in providing water for the men and horses of an entire Mounted Corps. Fortunately our stay was not a long one. We moved out on night of 30th. The big scrap started before daylight on 31st. Tel-el-Saba, one of a range of hills about 1,000 feet high, and three miles east of Beersheba, was found to be held in strength. This was a foregone conclusion, as a glance at the map will show. Time being all important, the natural thing to do seemed to be to envelop the position and march round it to the east and get astride the Beersheba—Jerusalem road. However, the 3rd Regiment, and a regiment of N.Z.M.R. Brigade were sent straight at it to make a frontal attack. Our C.O. was detached to command Brigade Advance Headquarters, and Major Markwell assumed command of the Regiment. 1st and 2nd Regiments were ordered down on to the plain to support 3rd Regiment if necessary and also to guard their left flank which was threatened. Tel-el-Saba was so well defended by machine guns (which our field batteries could make no impression on) that the frontal attack could make no headway. About 1400 2nd Regiment was ordered to come into action on the left of the 3rd, and to co-operate in the attack on Tel-el-Saba. We went in at the gallop and reached some mud huts about 800 yards from our objective. Here we dismounted and sent led horses back. Our 13 pounder guns, though well served, were making not the slightest impression on the Turkish redoubts; and additional guns were sent up to assist. That old veteran Lieut. Wasson was wounded, and while being carried away a shell again seriously wounded him, and killed one of the stretcher-bearers.

Our coming in on the left of the 3rd Regiment drew the bulk of the defenders' garrison that way, thus, though we could not advance ourselves, enabling the N.Z.M.R. Brigade on the right to push up to the Turkish position; but not before we had sustained our heaviest casualty. About 1630, an enemy shrapnel bursting low, had killed Major Markwell. The loss of that most gallant officer was irreparable. The following is an extract from Routine Order which expressed the opinion of all—"The C.O. desires to place on record the severe loss to the Regiment, in the death of Major W. E. Markwell, D.S.O. His loyal and devoted services to the Regiment since its formation were exemplary. His courage and energy in the field, his ability and conscientiousness as an administrator, his frank and generous nature, as a comrade, combined to mark him as one of the finest soldiers in the A.I.F., and his untimely death before reaching his prime, while in temporary command of the Regiment, is a heavy blow to this unit in particular, and to the A.I.F. as a whole."

Tel-el-Saba having fallen, two troops, under Lieuts. Weller and Anderson were attached to 1st Regiment which was now advancing dismounted against the town of Beersheba itself. It was now nearly dusk, and though we had not yet gained the ancient city, the Turks realising they were surrounded, were preparing to fly. Most of their guns had already been pulled out. The outer works to south, and west of the city had fallen to the 20th Corps. The 1st Regiment had almost reached Beersheba when the 4th Brigade was sent in at the gallop, they and the 1st Regiment almost dead heating into different quarters of the town. The Brigade, less one regiment, assembled in Wadi Saba that night. Our casualties for this engagement were as follows:—

Killed: One officer and one other rank.

Died of Wounds: One other rank.

Wounded: Three officers and 13 other ranks.

Various awards were made for gallantry in the field.

We wondered why our transport did not arrive, but next morning found it had suffered very severly indeed in a bombing raid by enemy 'planes. The whole transport of Desert Corps, some miles back along the road, had been attacked. As luck would have it, the 2nd. Regiment suffered most heavily. The following were our casualties:—

Killed: Five other ranks.

Died of Wounds: One officer and six other ranks.

Wounded: Seven other ranks.

Twenty-two draught horses were killed. We also lost valuable stores. This naturally delayed our subsequent movements somewhat.

On November 2, the Regiment moved out at mid-night with Brigade, to attack a strong enemy force which was entrenched at Khuweilfeh, guarding the only water in the neighbourhood, and holding up the advance of the mounted troops in their sweep round the Gaza line. The 1st Regiment was advance guard and were ordered to attack about 0730. Our "C" Squadron, under Capt. Evans, was sent to occupy Ras-el-Nagb, a commanding and rocky hill, and really the key to the situation. "A" Squadron, under Capt. Handley, was sent to support the 1st Regiment, on their right. At 1300 orders were received to concentrate the Regiment near 1st Regiment Headquarters, but as "C" Squadron were then being attacked at Ras-el-Nagh, it was not possible to withdraw them till their relief by the 5th Mounted Brigade at 1600. The Regiment concentrated for a combined attack with 1st Regiment by 1700. As it had been ascertained that the enemy was in much greater strength than had been supposed and as the 1st Regiment had sustained heavy casualties during the day, the order for the assault was cancelled at 1830 and the Brigade withdrew to Beersheba to water. The 5th Yeomanry Brigade took our place at holding the enemy there till a Brigade of Infantry and sufficient guns could arrive to dislodge him.

Our casualties for the day were:—

Died of Wounds: One other rank.

Wounded: One officer and six other ranks.

On November 5, Major Birkbeck, who had been acting as laison officer between 20th Corps and Desert Mounted Corps, resumed duty with Regiment and took over Second-in-Command, Major Stodart resuming command of "C" Squadron. Lieut. Pledger had been appointed Adjutant, on evacuation of Capt. Ellwood.

On November 6, though Khuweilfeh had not fallen, and was still threatening, it was decided to push on past it, and ignore it; as our main objective, the garrison of Gaza, was in danger of being missed through the delay. Accordingly, at 1645, we received orders to form the advance guard to Brigade and to march to Khirbet-Um-el-Bakr, near Sheria, and distant about 12 miles over a very rough track. We arrived about midnight and were joined by the rest of the Division. A rough outpost line was taken over from Dorset Yeomanry, and at dawn we pushed forward again.

Tel-el-Sheria had fallen during the night to the 60th Infantry Division. At 0600 we got touch and exchanged shots with enemy cavalry and shortly afterwards we came under artillery fire. We were ordered to water in Wadi Sheria as it was likely that we would encounter very dry stages ahead. The facilities in Wadi Sheria were very poor, there were only scattered wells, spread over two miles, with capacity for 6 to 8 horses at a time. We were thus scattered, when the order came to advance on Amiedat, a large enemy depot, 4½ miles distant. After a short inevitable delay in collecting the Regiment, we advanced on Amiedat at the trot, capturing it with about 300 prisoners, and a huge quantity of ammunition and other booty. We just missed capturing a battery that had been worrying us all the morning.

Our rapid advance relieved the pressure on the Infantry, who were moving north from Sheria. From Amiedat we pushed a patrol towards Jemmama, but they were held up by a force of about 300 in position near Tel-Abu-Dilakh. On 7th, Gaza fell, and the Mounted Corps was still some distance from the line of retreat of that garrison. On morning of November 8, the Regiment moved towards Jemmama, with orders to fill in the gap between 2nd and 3rd Brigades and to keep touch with them as it was reported that the enemy were trying to break through and escape that way. The 1st and 3rd Regiments were absent on detached duty. We gained touch with both 2nd and 3rd Brigades who were occupying defensive positions. At 1300 we received orders to attack Jemmama where there was known to be a good water supply. This was taken at 1630. We were then relieved by 3rd Regiment who had arrived from Amiedat—"A" Squadron of 2nd Regiment took over duties of 3rd Regiment at Amiedat; as the enemy force at Khuweilfeh still threatened our communications and rear. The Regiment watered and bivouaced for the night at Jemmama. Rations had been getting very short, but a day's supply was received during the night. At daylight on 9th, the Brigade advanced via Simsim and Burien, to the ancient city of El Mejdel, near Ascalon, where we arrived at 1300. During this march we found what good execution had been done by our battery (Inverness R.H.A.—then commanded by Capt. Balley) on the previous day; a long column of enemy transport having been washed out and abandoned. "C" Squadron remained at El Mejdel; Major Stodart having been appointed Military Governor.

Touch was regained with the enemy, by 3rd Regiment who were now leading, near Esdud about eight miles north of Mejdel. The Brigade occupied the old town and requisitioned on the inhabitants for rations, our own supply wagons being by this time, many miles in rear. We were now the leading Brigade and in touch with the enemy rear-guard, the delay at Khuweilfeh having prevented our reaching the enemy line of retreat from Gaza, till too late to inflict much damage.

From Esdud, Capt. McDougall was sent back to guide "A" Squadron up from Amiedat. "C" Squadron rejoined us at daylight on 11th, and the Regiment, less "A" Squadron, was sent to reconnoitre Wadi Sakerier and

Tel-el-Murre, and to report on watering facilities, etc.

Burka was held by the enemy in strength.

Excellent water was found in the Wadi.

Next morning Burka was attacked by 52nd Division and the Brigade was ordered to co-operate till relieved by 8th Mounted Brigade.

We were pulled out at dusk, and bivouaced at Haririyeh, where we had live sheep issued as rations.

On 13th we moved to Yebna and took up outpost line on left of 52nd Division, from that ancient city to the sea. The enemy were still retiring and we had an uneventful night. Leaving Yebna at daylight, we marched through Zernuka to Ras Deiran, where we were held up for a while by heavy shell fire.

We were now getting into more civilised country and movements were becoming restricted to roads; something quite new for us. The N.Z.M.R. Brigade were on our left this night and had a couple of very stiff fights at Nebi Kunda, Wadi Hanein, and Richon-le-Zion. Our "B" Squadron was sent to support them at the former place at 2000. They rejoined us early next morning.

At 0800, the Regiment moved through 1st and 3rd Regiments, who had formed the outpost line the previous night, with orders to "occupy tactical positions towards Ramleh." This was done; and reported; and without further orders, "C" Squadron pushed into Ramleh, an old Crusader town, and "B" Squadron pushed a patrol beyond it, astride the railway north of Ludd (old biblical Lod). We were the first British troops into both cities. We took two officers and 27 other ranks prisoners, besides much grain, ammunition and stores, including aeroplanes, etc. "B" and "C" Squadron furnished the outpost line north and north east of Ludd that night. Ludd is 12 miles north east of Yebna, and 34 miles north east of Gaza.

Next morning (16th) we occupied Safiriyeh and camped. On the 17th, "B" Squadron patrolled as far as the Jewish Settlement of Mulebbis, reporting six oil engines and 40 wells there, also good water in Wadi Nahr-el-Auja. Our patrols were driven out of Mulebbis next day and that town and Bald Hill were occupied by enemy in strength.

We were now coming to country favourable to the enemy and where it was expected he would make a stand. On 18th we moved to Yasur and took up outpost line, Ibn Ibrak—Sakia—Kafr Ana inclusive; the whole Regiment in the line—no supports.

On 17th the N.Z.M.R. Brigade had occupied Jaffa; and as we were keeping touch with them on their right, some of us entered that important town on 20th; on which day also, we got a big parcel mail.

During the operation covering the period October 31 to date, our casualties in horses were. Killed, died and destroyed, 86, evacuated wounded and sick, 105, It was during these Beersheba operations, that mules were first used by us in lieu of draught horses, and highly successful they proved.

On 21st the Brigade was pulled back for a short spell. Our transport and supply people were having difficulty in feeding us so far away, and though the railway was being pushed through Gaza and onwards, as rapidly as possible, the troops in the front line had to be reduced to a minimum to make the supply proposition reasonable. We therefore moved back to Haririyeh till 27th, on which day we m oved up again to Yebna, whence the Regiment was detached from Brigade, and reported to 54th Division Headquarters, Ramleh. We were then attached to 162 Infantry Brigade at Ludd.

The enemy had now taken up a definite and strong line as follows: Nahr-el-Auja—Bald Hill—Rantieh—Jimzu—Shilto and Bethlehem, thus covering Jerusalem; and the 54th Division were in active touch with him north of Ludd, at Rantieh, about six and a half miles distant. On night of 28th, Lieut Jones took a patrol through enemy's line and located his second line.

Our orders were to get thoroughly in touch with the whole of the sector held by 54th Division so as to be able to reinforce any part of it, and if necessary counter attack, by day or night. Officers were therefore busily employed locating tracks, etc. At night we assisted in improving the line, digging and wiring so close to enemy's position that work in daylight was impossible. No. 902. Sergt. G. Young was seriously wounded during this work.

This went on till December 12, when we rejoined the Brigade at Ayun Kara. On December 4, Major Birkbeck temporarily took over command of the Regiment, and Capt. S. N. McLean (Australian Engineers) was attached to us for duty. On December 9th, the enemy having been almost man-oeuvred out of Jerusalem, by the 20th Corps and part of Australian Division, that wonderful old city was captured by the 60th Division, under Major-General Shea, after sharp fighting, particularly at Nebi Samwil, and Mount of Olives. This compelled a considerable modification of the enemy front. His Right remained firm at Tabsor, his Centre was secure in the hills, but his Left was withdrawn up the Nablus Road, just north of Nebi Samwil, curving thence south east to the northern end of the Dead Sea, and including Jerico and the whole of the Jordan Valley.

With a view view to the Brigade participating in an attack by 52nd and 54th Divisions. the C.O. and Squadron Leaders inspected front line trenches near Bald Hill on December 15. On 17th, the Regiment, less "A" Squadron, took over part of line near Hill 765, from 4th Scottish Fusiliers. "A" Squadron were attached to 1st Regiment and held in reserve. Brigade frontage was from Hill 265 to Birket-el-Jamas, both inclusive. Our horses had been sent back to Ayun Kara (Richon-le-Zion). The weather was very wet.

On 21st, we were shelled, and at 1730 we relieved the 3rd Regiment on Hill 265. All was quiet until our bombardment of Bald Hill commenced, when we were heavily shelled; but only sustained one casualty—No. 1155. Tpr. W. J. Davies, mortally wounded. The main position was captured by the 54th Division. The 52nd Division effected an important advance nearer the sea, crossing the Wadi Nahr-el-Auja, which was in flood; and securing good positions on the north bank, forcing the enemy's right flank back five miles, thereby securing Jaffa from shell fire.

On December 23, the operation being over, we withdrew to Ayun Kara, where we spent Christmas. Owing to the excellent parcel post arrange-ments, our Xmas mail was waiting for us, including parcels from Regimental Comforts Fund, Brisbane, and the A.I.F. Comforts Fund, which were very acceptable.

On 26th we were withdrawn to Esdud for a short spell. This meant a march back of 20 miles. The weather was execrable, the black soil plains, devoid of roads, were converted by the rain into swamps. The Transport had an awful time. The 2nd Regiment wagons were the only ones of the Brigade that got through.

On January 4, with six machine guns attached, we left for Neby Kunda, en route to relieve the 4th Light Horse Brigade at Midieh and Nalin, about eight miles east of Ludd and about 30 miles from Esdud. The outpost line was situated in some very rough country. "B" Squadron was allotted the right of our sector, in touch with the 1st Leinster's (10th Division), "C" Squadron was on the left, and in touch with the 75th Division. "A" Squadron was in support.

The next week was taken up in building "sangars" (it was impossible to dig), patrolling, bombing practices, etc. We made a very good job of the defences and then started road making. Our zig-zags down the precipitous hill sides, (made under the supervision of Lieut. Weidman, Engineer Officer) were engineering triumphs—in our own estimation at least—and we were very proud to have the road ready for wheel traffic by January 19, when the position was inspected by B.G.G.S. (Brig-General Howard Vyse) on behalf of the Corps Commander. He congratulated the Regiment on the work done. The weather was bitterly cold and wet, so that the normal rations issued seemed quite inadequate.

On 20th we were relieved by the Canterbury Mounted Rifles, and marched to Divisional Bivouac Area at Richon, reaching there at 1230 on January 21. Refresher courses for all Officers and N.C.O.'s were started there. On February 2 we gave a demonstration before the Corps and Divisional Commanders of an "Attack in depth, by a mounted Regiment." General Chauvel fully approved of the manoeuvre.

An advance eastwards to seize the Jordan Valley and ultimately turn the enemy's left flank, was now spoken of; but these operations, extending as they do over the best part of a very strenuous year, deserve a chapter to themselves.

Standing: Lt. L. B. Guiren, M.C.
Sitting: Lt. J. M. Wills, M.M., Capt. Fred Evans, M.C., and the Regimental Mascot
Jack Hanna (See Appendix)

CHAPTER VIII.

JORDAN VALLEY AND THE HILLS OF MOAB

ON February 16, 1918, at 100, the Brigade left Richon en route for Jerusalem. We arrived at Junction Station at 1530, and camped. The next stages were Zakaryya, and El Khudr, a small village near Bethlehem. The N.Z.M.R. Brigade had preceded us. The operation with the object of capturing Jerico was entrusted to 53rd and 60th Divisions, with Anzac Division (less 2nd Brigade). On February 18, Brigadier-General Cox having returned, Lieut.-Colonel Bourne relinquished command of the Brigade and resumed command of the Regiment—Squadron Leaders being "A" Capt. Brown, "B" Capt. Evans and "C" Major Stodart.

On morning of 19th, we filed through Bethlehem by a very tedious track, arriving at Beit Obeid at 1400, where we watered. The track was very rough and in some places so steep and narrow, that leading in single file was necessary. After a halt for lunch and feed-up, we advanced about two miles towards Muntar, which had been taken by the Infantry the previous day, where we drew rations and halted till about 1900. The difficulty of the further advance was accentuated by darkness; but Muntar was reached without serious mishap, and the column halted here till shortly before dawn. Fortunately some ancient cisterns, containing good water, were found among the hills. It was also possible to water a small proportion of the horses by bucket without hanging up the Column, as its progress was necessarily slow. Early on the morning of the 20th our guns could be heard pounding Jebell Ekteif and Talat-ed-Dumm, to the north prior to the assault of those places by the Infantry. Our path to the Jordan Valley ran through some very difficult country near Nebi Musa. The advance in many places could only be made in half sections, the path was steep and commanded everywhere by precipitous cliffs. It was an ideal place for a rear guard to hang up a large force; and as the enemy had a mountain battery as well as several machine-guns it was not to be wondered at, that the advance guard (N.Z.M.R. Brigade) was unable to make any appreciable progress in daylight. Information having been received that another track down into the Jordan Valley existed further south, the 1st Brigade pushed round by it reaching the vicinity of Nebi Musa on the easterly side before day on 21st. The N.Z.M.R. Brigade had pushed on during the night from the west side of Nebi Musa and found it evacuated. The 2nd Regiment had been detailed to afford protection to the 3rd Regiment, while the latter attacked Nebi Musa from the east, but the evacuation of the position having been reported, the most northerly troops (a patrol of the 3rd Regiment and "C" Squadron of the 2nd Regiment, under Major C.C. Stodart, "M.C.") pushed into Jericho together. After watering in the Wadi Kelt, which was flowing strongly, the Regiment pushed patrols to the Wadi Obeideh, 4 miles north of Jericho; and to the Jordan; subsequently taking up the outpost line from El Ghoraniyeh to mouth of Aujah, a distance of almost eight miles. Daylight patrols, under Capt. McLean and Lieut.

53

King ("C" Squadron) got into active touch with the enemy; Corporal Apelt being mentioned for especially good work, and afterwards awarded the Military Medal. Sergt Schmidt, later took a patrol to the Jordan to ascertain whether two enemy guns, alleged to have been abandoned on the west flank, were actually there. No trace of them could be seen and enemy position at bridge head was reported to be strong. Day posts were found by this Regiment for February 22. These were shelled at intervals through the day, and were withdrawn at 1800. After dark the Brigade started on the return journey to Bethlehem, bivouac being reached at 0430 on the 23rd after a miserably cold night march. The Regiment suffered no casualties, but the operations were severe on horses owing to the very rough going and the cold; two were killed, four wounded, three died of exhaustion, 79 evacuated on account of lameness and general exhaustion. The Regiment captured 27 prisoners during the operation. On the 24th the Regiment spelled at Bethlehem and opportunity was given to those who wished to visit the places of interest here and at Jerusalem. The journey to the old bivouac near Richon-le-Zion occupied the 25th and 26th instant. To return there gave us something of the feeling of home; partly no doubt because some tents, most of our baggage, etc., had been left there—but partly because of the beauty of the place. The almond trees had burst into bloom, giving added loveliness to country that already boasted acres of dark green orange groves brightened with golden fruit; of severely pruned vines set on the chocolate ridges in rows with mathematical rgularity; hedged lanes, full of bird life, and of fields tinted with white snowdrops and narcissi, scarlet anemonies, yellow marguerites, purple iris and a score of others. Last, but not least, the plantations of blue gums, tall, graceful, and very familiar, gave the place an atmosphere that carried the thoughts of more than one man many miles away.

By March 5, the Regiment had been reinforced by both men and horses, and moved out with the Brigade en route for Beitin, on the Nablus road and north of Jerusalem arriving there on 8th, having voted for the Queensland elections during the journey. The Brigade formed the reserve. On 9th, the Regiment received orders to be ready to move out to Tel-Asur at an hour's notice. Capt. McLean and Lieut Sinton were sent to reconnoitre the road. On 10th we received our first intimation that an attack east of the Jordan was contemplated, Lieut. Weller and Lieut. Sinton being detailed together with Officers of the 3rd Regiment to reconnoitre crossings over the Jordan, and the hills beyond. Valuable information was gained although they were unable to cross the river owing to the Turks holding the fords. On 13th the Brigade moved to Bethlehem, receiving orders to conceal themselves within the olive groves. The weather was bitterly cold with continuous rain, so much so that the men had to be billeted; this being the first time this had been possible. The rain interfered considerably with the higher commands plans, in that the Jordan River and tributaries were in high flood. However, on the 20th the Brigade moved out under cover of darkness en route for the Jordan Valley, ("A" Squadron under Capt. McDougall advanced guard) arrived at Nebi Musa at 2100 on 21st. The Jordan was in such a high state of flood that the Engineers had not been able to erect a bridge over it. The Regiment, therefore, was forced to conceal itself in the numerous hollows in the vicinity of Moses Monument until 23rd, when we moved to Makhadet Hajla. The Anzac Mounted Divisional Engineers had thrown a pontoon bridge across the river after much difficulty, this being the first British military bridge over the Jordan.

The Bridgehead was held by 60th Infantry Division who pushed the enemy well across the Valley. The crossing was effected and the following dispositions, as per orders, made: "A" Squadron under Capt. McDougall moving down river to secure Ain Sueime, "B" Squadron, under Capt. Handley, moving out to secure Salha. Both sent out patrols several miles without opposition from the enemy who withdrew rapidly into the mountains. At 1800 a line of Cossack posts was formed holding the line already occupied. At 2100 the Regiment was ordered to re-join the Brigade which had crossed the river later in the day and were some miles north. During this march in the dark R.S.M. Crain was injured through his horse falling upon him. On joining up with Brigade on 24th the Regiment took over the outpost from the 3rd Regiment, who were holding from Jordan river to the foothills, about four miles north of the bridge, and linking up with 1st Regiment. On 25th the Regiment advanced its lines about six miles to cover the track from Umm Es Shert to Es Salt. During the advance the Regiment was subjected to artillery fire and some opposition from enemy infantry posts but gained positions covering the road. The 3rd Regiment was ordered to push on up the precipitous goat tracks to Es Salt. On 27th the Regiment relieved 1st Regiment, the dispositions being: "B" Squadron north of Dadi Ralem, "C" Squadron Umm Es Shert, "A" Squadron in reserve. "C" Squadron was ordered to secure high ground north of Umm Es Shert and in doing so had the following casualties.

Killed: One other rank.

Wounded: Four other ranks.

Orders were then received to occupy Mafid Jozele, a high flat-topped ridge commanding Umm Es Shert crossing over the Jordan and the flat country to the foothills, which threatened our long thin line and consequently the 3rd Regiment's communications. "A" Squadron under Capt. McDougall was ordered to attack. He sent out an officer's patrol, to ascertain the enemy strength, which succeeded in gaining the main ridge, but owing to the enemy being heavily reinforced, our attack was not pressed.

On the 28th fresh dispositions were made by Brigade; the 1st Regiment holding Umm Es Shert, thus relieving our "C" Squadron; and the whole 2nd Regiment holding Wadi Ralem and Es Salt road from foothills to plateau above.

Water was discovered in Wadi Ralem and Engineers were soon busy developing it.

At 1000 a large enemy force was observed marching across our front from the Jisr Ed Damie crossing (eight miles further up the Jordan) towards Es Salt, with its flank on Wadi Ishkarara.

The Regiment was forced back through enemy gaining high ground to east of its position, and withdrew to stronger position about a quarter of a mile south, which denied the water to the enemy and still covered the road. At the same time, "A" Squadron was pushed right up on to the high ground thus covering the head of the Es Salt road and the plateau beyond, a second line being formed in the rear as it appeared very probable that we would be attacked in force. The enemy's main force moved eastward leaving a strong force to guard his rear and mask us. On 29th an attempt was made to regain the ground lost on the previous day, but we were again outflanked by superior numbers. Beyond constant sniping, no further attempt was made by the enemy to dislodge us until noon on 30th, when we were subjected to artillery fire from enemy battery situated on Mafid Jozele, and again at 1600, but without causing much damage.

At this stage the general situation was none too good. The main attack on Amman was making but little progress. The Turks were reinforcing, and the only British Force holding the Jordan Valley to the northwards, was 1st Brigade, less 3rd Regiment; thus with about 500 men in the line, the 1st and 2nd Regiments were holding a vital position over four miles in length, the piercing of which would have meant the cutting of communications of the three Divisions operating to the east of the Jordan. Realising this, a battalion of Infantry was sent to support us. They occupied the second line we had started to prepare, about 1½ miles in rear. The 31st saw the position unchanged and quiet, other than for intermittent sniping and artillery fire by the enemy.

Orders were received to detail an officer and six men to report to 60th Division Headquarters for instructions. Lieut Sinton was detailed for the duty, which turned out to be a patrol to Madeba.

This proved to be an exciting trip, as the envoys who came from Madeba and were returning there, were found, by Lieut. Sinton, with their throats cut, about half way to that place, evidently murdered by enemy agents. On arrival at Madeba, Lieut. Sinton's party was welcomed by the inhabitants and made the recipients of gifts, and there was general rejoicing over the first British troops to enter the town.

No definite information having been received from the Division, and water becoming scarce, all horses were ordered back, under command of Major Birkbeck, to the watering area about four miles from the front line.

On April 2, information was received that the attack on Amman had failed, and that the Column was withdrawing. An attempt to interrupt the withdrawal by striking at our communications, and so confirming their success, seemed the obvious enemy plan; but our movements were too rapid for him to put it in execution. By 1400 the main body of the Column had reached the valley; and at 1430 the Regiment, acting as rear-guard, started to move south, followed by the enemy cavalry. They, however, kept at a sufficiently respectful distance to avoid actual conflict with us; but our armoured cars succeeded in ambushing a party of them. Their guns, too, failed to make full use of their opportunities. The whole force successfully re-crossed the Jordan at Ghoraniyeh Bridge-Head, which was held by 180th Infantry Brigade

On April 3rd the Brigade, with 5th Regiment attached, took over Ghoraniyeh Bridge-Head from the 180th Brigade (Infantry). The position was organised in four equal sections, each of which had been held by a battalion, which found its own supports.

It surprised us somewhat, therefore to find that though the weakest

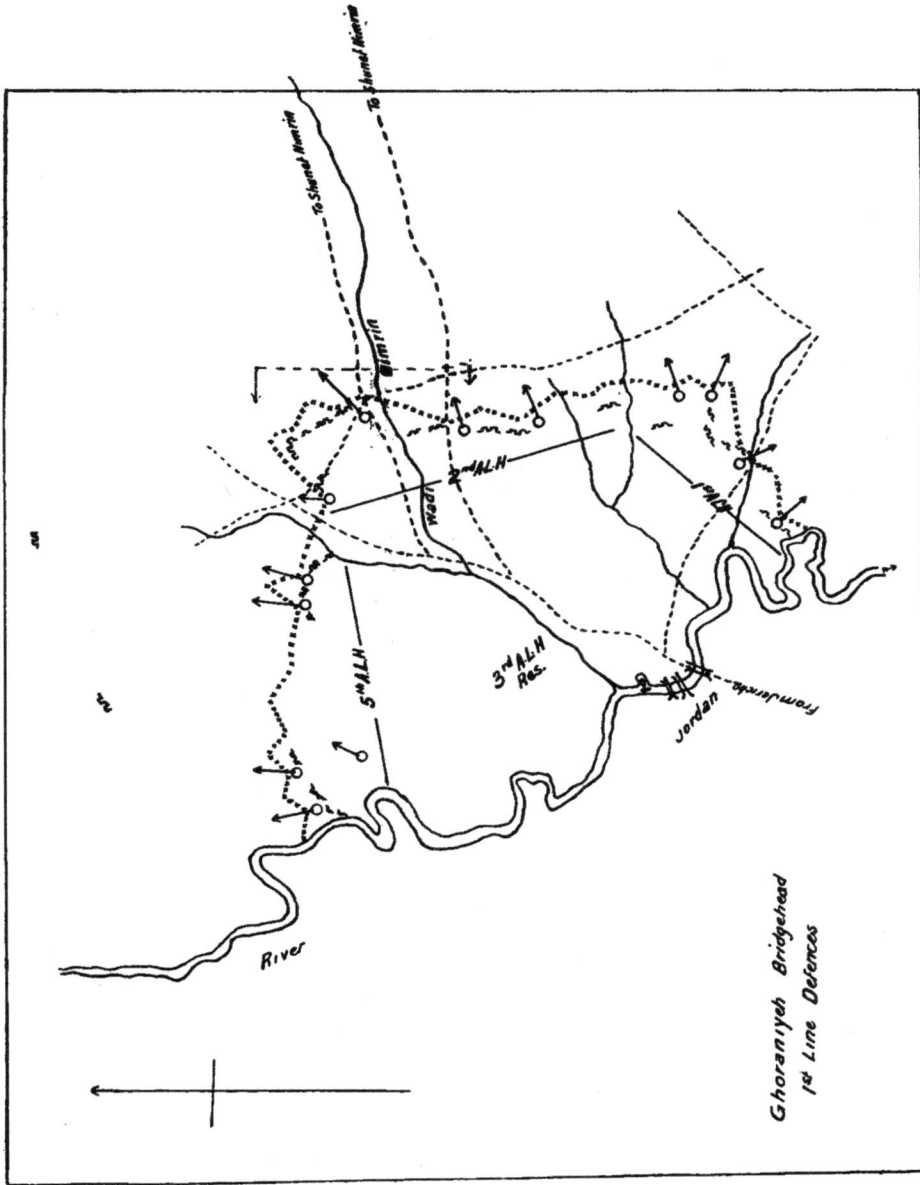

Frontage of Turkish attack on 11th April, 1918, along Wadi Nimrin from the East is shewn thus

·······→

Scale.—2in.—1 mile.

—Sketch by R. F. Bourne, Lieut R.E.

Regiment numerically we were given two sections to hold. One section on the right was allotted to the 1st Regiment and one on the left to the 5th Regiment. The 3rd Regiment was held in reserve.

Owing to the length of frontage to be held, all three squadrons were put into the line. We made up for the weakness in numbers by working our hardest to improve and consolidate the position. Owing to the great heat and the kind attention of the enemy gunners, we did practically the whole of our digging and wiring at night and in the early morning. By dint of keeping constantly at it we had just completed our wire with single apron, by the night of April 10 and very fortunate this proved.

Our patrols were constantly in touch with enemy patrols both Infantry and Cavalry. The Turks had fortifed the naturally strong position at Shunet Nimrin, completely blocking the Es Salt road where it enters the mountains, and were thus in strength only four miles off.

Our patrols took a few prisoners: Deserters, too, used to trickle in.

The enemy attacked on April 11. The C/O's report extracted from the War Diary is as follows:—

"At about 0430 on 11th instant one of our patrols came into con-"tact with what appeared to be an enemy patrol in vicinity of Hut on "left bank of Wadi Nimrin, 1400 yards in front of our position; shots "were exchanged and our patrols promptly got word back. Advice "was sent immediately to Brigade Head Quarters. A few minutes later "about 100 Turks could be seen advancing along and on both banks of "Wadi Nimrin, and I reported to the Brigade Major that the enemy "was apparently making a reconnaissance in force. As the light im-"proved, however, it became evident that he was in considerably greater "strength—many waves in extended formation could be seen advancing "—I then reported that enemy intended attacking with estimated "strength of 1000 on frontage of about 600 yards, with centre on Wadi "Nimrin. The enemy was favoured by semi darkness and had excellent "natural cover; and near road No. 5 reached to within 100 yards of our "wire, when their advance was dealt with most effectually along their "whole front by our M.G. and Hotchkiss Rifles. I instructed Squadron "leaders to reserve fire as much as possible, and not to disclose their "strength. Enemy was evidently surprised to find our wiring complete "and fire power so strong. Artillery co-operation was asked for by "me; and obtained about 0550. Both 60-pounders and Field Batteries "did excellent work; and materially assisted in repelling the ad-"vance. The 5th L.H. Regiment gave valuable aid in bringing fire to "bear on enemy's right flank. At about 0600 I accompanied the "Brigadier to observation post on right of my position. Careful ob-"servation of enemy from here gave his strength at 2,000 which was "confirmed by statements of prisoners subsequently. Enemy by this "time had moved 9 M.G. into good positions, raked our trenches and "searched roads etc., in back areas; and a considerable number of "snipers who had dug themselves in before it was light, kept up heavy "and accurate fire on our position. The enemy also shelled us throughout "the day with 4.2 and 77 M. guns, though these only succeeded in in-"flicting casualties amongst the horses. Owing to this Regiment hold-

"ing two sectors of the line my whole force was employed in the
"trenches; one squadron of the 3rd L.H. Regiment with two M.G. was
"therefore sent to me. I kept the squadron in support till 1200 when it
"rejoined its Regiment being replaced by one squadron 5th L.H. Regi-
"ment

"The two M.G. were put into line at once, in the sector threatened,
"one of the original guns having been put out of action in the morn-
"ing. It soon became evident that the enemy had missed any chance
"of success he might have had, by waiting till it was light, as we were
"well able to stop any further advance by our small arm fire; and our
"artillery was dealing severely with his supports. Our snipers also to a
"great extent counteracted those of the enemy. At 1245 mounted sorties
"were made by the 3rd L.H. Regiment from our left; and by one
"squadron 1st L.H. Regiment from our right—the artillery at the same
"time increasing their rate of fire. I had arranged to advance part of
"my regiment dismounted had this manoeuvre succeeded in forcing the
"enemy to retire, but he had taken steps to meet such a movement by
"his depth and number of M.G. employed; and he was able to hold
"tenaciously to his ground, no rearward movement being observed.
"At dark the enemy became active and it seemed possible that he would
"renew the attack—lights being seen and many voices heard in the
"Wadi at intervals till 0300 next morning. We kept touch by patrols
"who reported half hourly. At 0400 we raided and captured the
"nearest enemy posts; and our patrols following up, discovered that
"the main body had withdrawn; they pursued and captured some prison-
"ers—who apparently formed part of the rearguard.

"Great credit is due to Captains S. N. McLean and W. J. Brown
"against whose posts the attack developed, for the manner in which
"they handled their squadrons and rendered, their reports etc. Lieut.
"H. C. Kemp 1st L.H.M.G.S. did splendid work, which is the subject of
"a special report to his C.O. I regret he was severely wounded about
"0725. The artillery co-operation was good and reflects great credit on
"the F.O.O.'s one of whom was mortally wounded. The following
"casualties were suffered by my regiment. Killed 6 O.R. Wounded
"17 O.R., two of whom have since died. Enemy casualties on my front
"were as follows. Killed 151, actual count. Wounded and taken prison-
"ers 25 O.R. Estimated wounded removed by enemy 500. Unwounded
"prisoners taken by this Regiment three officers and 63 O.R., 11 Arabs,
"eight Armenians. The following enemy material was forwarded by
"us to Ordnance—Rifles 101; Bayonets 43.

"We expended 38,000 rounds of S.A.A. including M.G. ammunition
during the operation."

Our next task was to bury the large number of enemy dead outside
our wire. Our machine gunners had done great execution. On the other
hand the enemy had, we found, brought up over-head cover etc., for their
M. gun positions and these had been so well constructed that our artillery
had not damaged them.

The attack had been launched solely against the two sections held by
the 2nd Regiment.

On April 15 one Squadron and one Company Indian Imperial Service Troops were attached to the Regiment for front line experience, (viz. Hyderabad Lancers and Alwar Infantry). Very keen and capable troops they proved to be.

On 18th we handed Ghoraniyeh Bridge Head over to the 20th Indian Imperial Service Brigade—our Brigade moving into reserve—though we continued to supply the patrols.

On April 29 the second series of operations against Es Salt and Amman began.

The general plan of attack was as follows: The 60th Infantry Division with one Brigade Mounted Troops attached, were to make a frontal attack on the Shunet Nimrin and El Haud positions which were held by the enemy in strength. They were to force their way up the main Es Salt Road. The Australian Mounted Division plus 1st Light Horse Brigade were to move northwards up the Jordan Valley and attack the enemy's right, by the Nablus-Es Salt and Umm Es Shert—Es Salt tracks, which the Turks appeared to consider were impracticable for large bodies of mounted troops.

The 4th L.H. Brigade was entrusted with the important role of seizing and holding the Jisr Ed Damie crossing over the Jordan to prevent the enemy taking our attacking column in flank and rear.

The King of the Hedjaz promised to co-operate simultaneously, with 7000 men—but more of this anon.

The 4th and 3rd Brigades moved rapidly up the valley before dawn, drawing considerable fire especially from Mafid Jozele. Both Brigades reached their objectives in good time.

The 5th Cavalry Brigade (Yeomanry) made their way up the "Goat Track" or No. 7 road, (used by the 3rd Regiment in the previous operations) leading their horses in single file.

The 1st L.H. Brigade was employed in the morning watching the enemy at Mafid Jozele, but the 4th Brigade being in position, the higher command apparently considered one Squadron would be sufficient for this duty, consequently our Brigade (less one squadron, 1st L.H. Regiment) was ordered to follow the 5th Cavalry Brigade at 1500.

The steep climb of 2000 feet was negotiated without much trouble. Our horses were quite used to that sort of thing by now. From the crest of the plateau we got a good view of what was going on. It was found that the 60th Division had not been able to force the strong Turkish position at Shunet Nimrin and El Haud. The latter especially was a wonderfully good Artillery observation post for the enemy, enabling him to inflict severe damage on our Infantry—while our guns were not making the slightest impression on him, owing to want of observation.

The fact that the enemy still held these positions meant that our rear had to be protected. Accordingly "A" Squadron under Major Brown was left to guard the road by which we had just come. The Regiment less "A" Squadron proceded to within one mile of Es Salt.

Shortly after dawn on May 1, Major Brown reported that the enemy had established two posts immediately to the south of his position, and that they were manoeuvring with a view to cutting our communications.

The Regiment therefore moved back to supoprt him—and we were charged with the duty of keeping open the mountain track.

Dispositions to drive the enemy from his points of vantage were immediately made. Under covering fire from machine guns two troops under Lieuts. Joyner and Henderson succeeded in driving the enemy out and establishing themselves on the position which was henceforth known as "Joyner's Hill."

Two other posts on our left were too close to us to be convenient and Lieut King with twenty men was detailed to raid them by night.

The raid was brilliantly carried out—great credit being due to the leader—as owing to the very rough nature of the ground it was extremely difficult to locate the enemy in the dark, and surprise him. Five enemy were killed and four taken prisoners. The party also took seven horses, machine gun complete, belt filler, 10 rifles and 4000 rounds S.A.A. A Squadron of enemy who were supporting the post fled in disorder.

Our casualties were nil. Lieut King was awarded the M.C., and Sergeant Geddes the M.M. for this performance.

But no progress was being made in the main object of the operation. The King of the Hedjaz having consulted his oracle, decided that the day was not propitious for a battle. He therefore failed to co-operate with us in any way, with disastrous results for our column.

The 60th Division had been set a task far beyond their strength at Shunet Nimrin.

Lastly a strong Turkish force marching from Nablus had driven the 4th Brigade from Jisr Ed Damie with a loss of nine guns. The 4th Brigade were extended to their utmost in preventing this force from pushing right down the Jordan Valley and completely cutting off the Column on the plateau.

Under the circumstances, we had to confess to a second rebuff in this district. The Commander in Chief ordered the withdrawal, which was begun on the night of May 3. Delay in getting out would have been very risky for the whole Column—which even now had but one means of exit from the plateau, and which was quite unable to manoeuvre owing to the precipitous nature of the country.

Our C/O was detailed as O/C Rear Guard, and the Sherwood Rangers and Canterbury Mounted Rifles' (the latter Regiment dismounted) were also placed under his command. Our Regiment was wholly occupied at this time in keeping open Road No. 7 (the only track to the Valley which the Turks did not hold). For about three miles this road had to be guarded on both sides.

At 1900 on 3rd the whole force, with Christian-Refugees, Camel Convoys, Donkey Convoys, Mountain Batteries etc., began to withdraw along this narrow passage way that we were holding.

By 0800 the following morning the last troops passed through.

A section of the Regimental Staff under Saddler Sergeant Jorgensen were the last to leave the hight ground to the East of Road No. 7. They covered the withdrawal of two troops Sherwood Rangers. Sergt. Jorgensen and Private Brennan were wounded—the latter seriously. Both were dressed under fire by our M.O., Capt. Trinca and were safely removed.

Our Regiment then withdrew sector by sector, "B" Squadron moving through "A" Squadron and each in turn acting as rear guard and moving through "C" Squadron which held the crest of the plateau. The withdrawal of the rear guard was most orderly—the ground preventing the enemy from pursuing rapidly or on a broad front—and they missed their opportunity of cutting Road No. 7, though they shelled it. Enemy planes, too, bombed and machine gunned Rear Guard and Column.

The Regiment rejoined the Brigade at 1400 near Umm Es Shert and remained in support of 4th Brigade, ultimately covering its withdrawal at 2400.

At 0015 on 5th we formed part of the Rear Guard to 4th Brigade, reaching bivouac near Jericho at 0320.

Early in the mornings of 7th and 8th we were visited by seven enemy planes which bombed the whole bivouac area—but owing to the "scatter formation" which was now invariably adopted, we got off with only a few casualties among the horses.

On 10th the Regiment moved back to Talaat Ed Dumm in the hills between Jericho and Jerusalem, near which is the Inn of the Good Samaritan, marking the scene of the Biblical story. We rested here till the 16th when we moved to the vicinity of Solomon's Pools (between Hebron and Bethlehem.) While here we received very welcome consignments of comforts. The A.I.F. Canteen and Y.M.C.A. also established themselves without delay, so that we were able to live in comparative luxury.

The stay at Solomon's Pools was devoted to training—classes for N.C.O.'s Hotchkiss gunners, signallers, etc., were in full swing during the day and lectures were given in the evening.

Each day a number of men under an Officer visited the Holy places and spots of interest in and around Jerusalem and Bethlehem.

On June 6 the whole Brigade returned to the Jordan Valley. The prospect of spending mid-summer in that delightful spot, 1200 feet below sea level, and where the thermometer reached 128 degrees, was not a very pleasant one. We had been almost continuously in the Valley since February, but of course there were others there who now required relief, and we were much refreshed after our spell.

The Brigade took over the Auja Sector from the 4th Brigade. This included the Musallabah Salient—already famous for the gallant exploits of the Camel Corps there, and which was destined ultimately to be the scene of one of our most critical engagements.

The 1st and 3rd Regiments were put into the line—taking the right and left respectively. Their horses were sent about four miles to the rear. The 2nd Regiment was Brigade reserve. We had our horses with us, as it was realised that in the event of an attack, support would require to be afforded very rapidly.

One squadron was on duty each night, assisting the 1st and 3rd Regiments with the wiring and entrenching.

Our bivouac was shelled regularly each day—though the greatest care was taken to conceal the horses as far as possible.

On 30th the Regiment relieved the 1st Regiment on the right sector of the Brigade line.

The horses were sent back under Major Franklin who had just returned from Australia, and who took over the duties of Second in Command (Major Birkbeck being on special detached duty.)

For the past two months we had been steadily evacuating officers and men with malaria which they had contracted in the Valley, and as reinforcements were very few and far between, we went into line with a total strength of less than 230 rifles. We had one Section of 1st Machine Gun Squadron attached.

A word of explanation with a glance at the accompanying rough sketch should be of interest.

Musallabeh formed the apex of a salient in the northern line held by us; the base of the salient may be considered the Aujah River for, say 5000 yards. A similar salient in the Wadi Mallaha was held by the 2nd Brigade three miles to the East, while three to four miles to the west and rising 4000 feet above, were the Mountains forming the western side of the Jordan Gorge and the Eastern fringe of the precipitous country between Jerusalem and Nablus. These hills were held by the Turks who therefore had excellent observation of our movements. They had long range guns 4.2 and 5.9 on the hills; and field guns on Bakr Ridge and immediately to the north and north-east of us, with which they issued us a liberal daily ration of shells.

The positions we held were so rocky that trenching was always difficult and in many cases impossible—sangars in lieu of trenches had generally to be built. All movements, such as drawing rations, evacuating wounded, putting up wire and building sangars had to be by night.

We found the sangars very useful against machine gun and rifle fire when the attack came—but as places to live in when there is much H.E. flying about they cannot be recommended.

The position it will be seen could be shelled from three sides with excellent observation.

Its value to us lay in the fact that it was the most convenient high ground on our northern line giving good observations over the Valley on the right bank of the Jordan. It was a convenient "kicking off" place for possible operations to the north. It commanded a splendid water supply, viz. the Aujah River on which we were absolutely dependent. Finally, in the hands of the enemy it would have been a constant and serious menace to the whole British force in the Jordan Valley.

The key of the situation was Abu Tellul Ridge divided for convenience into 'right" and "left" sectors.

It was understood by all that on the first sign of an attack, the Reserve Regiment (now 1st Light Horse Regiment) would immediately garrison Abu Tellul. This was emphasised by General Chauvel and his B.G.G.S. when they inspected the position on July 13.

Each night we worked at improving the defensive works—one Squadron of the Reserve Regiment generally giving assistance.

In spite of the difficult digging, possies were constructed into which we dived when the daily shelling started, with such alacrity that our casualties were very light.

On July 4 at 2215 an enemy party attempted to raid Musallabeh but they only succeeded in driving in the listening post temporarily. The would be raiders got a warm reception and our listening posts were again in position a few minutes later. Two prisoners were taken.

On 6th at 0015 the enemy again attempted to raid Musallabeh, but were driven off by our standing patrol.

At 2000 that evening Sergt. Rogan took eight men out mounted, to raid a position thought to be held by the enemy a night, but found nobody there.

On July 7 "C" Squadron under Capt. McDougall exchanged places with "A" Squadron under Major Brown under cover of darkness.

From this onwards the artillery fire became more severe—from 200 to 300 shells falling on the positions daily, foreshadowing a possible attack.

A reserve water ration was stored in each post in empty petrol tins—but as an unlucky shell could easily have destroyed the reserve water for a whole post the C/O ordered a further emergency supply of two beer

'Musallabeh and Abu Tellul, 14th July, 1918

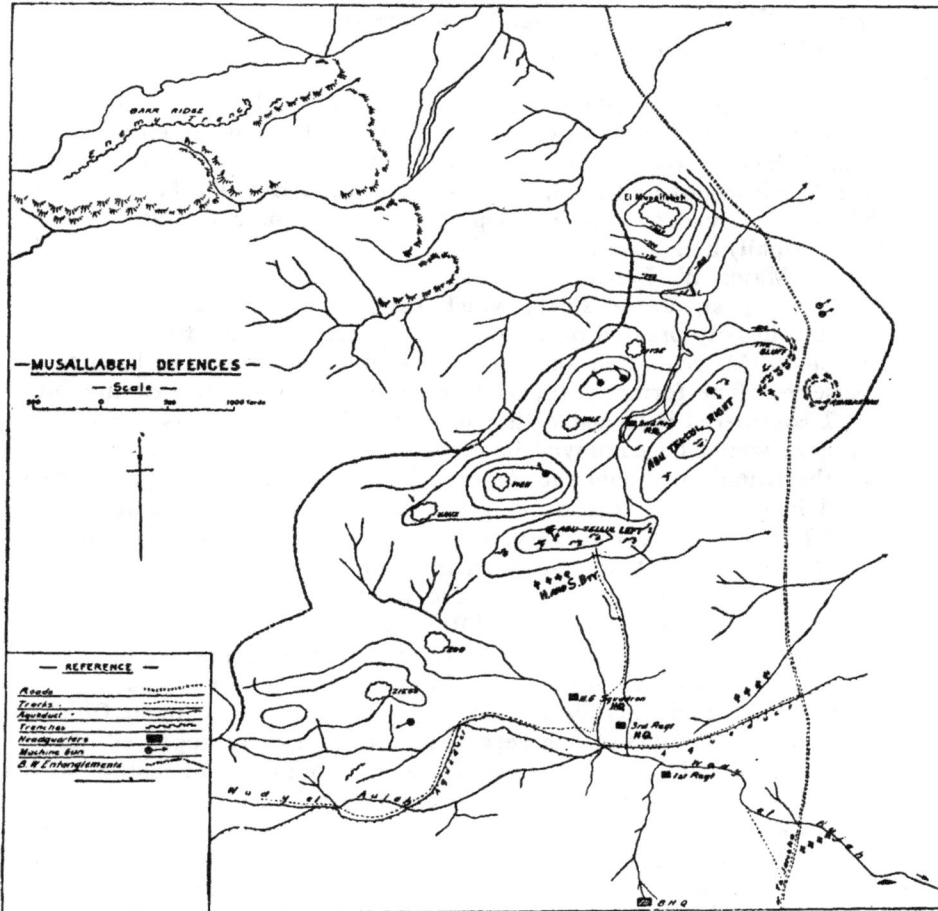

—Sketch by R. F. Bourne, Lieut. R.E.

bottles per man to be distributed over the positions. These were replenish-
ed nightly from the "fanatis" brought up by the ration camels. A few men
per Squadron were allowed to slip down to Wadi Aujah when things were
quiet to wash clothes and have a bath—not in the Wadi of course!

On July 13 considerable activity was observed among the enemy. Large
bodies of Infantry were seen moving in the vicinity of Wadi Bakr.
Divisional H.Q. advised that information had been received that the enemy
intended to retire. We were instructed to ascertain if this was so. The
shelling was so heavy, that it appeared that, in the rather unlikely event
of his retiring, Jacko did not intend to carry away any ammunition with
him! During the afternoon we observed that several new tents had been
erected at his Hospitals. So far from withdrawing this evidently meant an
attack, so the information was passed back and we prepared to give our
friends a warm reception.

The C/O's suggestion that one Squadron of the Reserve Regiment
should in anticipation of the attack, occupy its battle station Abu Tellul,
in rear of us (the Key of the situation) was rejected by B.H.Q.

The official report on the operation is transcribed from the War Diary
as follows:—

"The Regiment held the following posts which were designed for
"all round defence and between which it was admitted the enemy would
"push if he attacked during darkness, viz. Maskerah (Garrison 'B' Squad-
"ron less 2 troops under Capt. F. Evans, M.C., and plus 2 M.G.) Musell-
"abeh ('C' Squadron plus 1 troop 'B' Squadron under Capt. M. D.
"McDougall) and Vyse Post ('A' Squadron less 2 troops and plus 2 M.G.,
"under Major W. J. Brown). Vyse Post in addition found an advance
"bombing post, Vance Post; which had orders to fall back on Vyse
"Post if heavily pressed or as soon as day broke. Thus there were two
"troops of 'A' Squadron and 1 troop of 'B' Squadron in Regimental
"Reserve. The former bivouaced at Vyse Post, the latter at the Bluff,
"as I considered it probable that in event of attack at least part of my
"reserve would be employed in preventing the enemy gaining the key
"of the situation, should the Reserve Regiment (under Brigade orders)
"be delayed for any reason. Events more than justified this disposition.

"The Regiment was very weak being able to put only 250 rifles
"in the line. R.H.Q. was situated in Wadi Dhib immediately in rear
"of Vale Post, held by one troop 3rd Regt., the garrison of which was
"placed under my orders. On 13th instant increased enemy artillery
"activity, including registration of the position by a new battery of 5.9
"howitzers, warned us of the possibility of an attack. Enemy patrols were
"ported in the vicinity of the post during the night. About 0100 3rd
"Regiment and Mussalleheh reported that the enemy appeared to be
"massing, though at that time it was impossible to estimate his
"strength. At 0245 Vale Post reported enemy in strength outside their
"wire; about same time marked increase in enemy artillery fire was
"observed, which prevented movements being heard. Between 0200 and
"0300 all telephonic communications with squadrons and B.H.Q. was
"broken; my last report to Brigade was made shortly before 0300.

"As it appeared certain that my H.Q. would be overrun shortly, at

"0300 I sent the Signal Sergeant with a telephone to an alternative "battle station, prepared on Abu Tellul Station No. 3 Right and ordered "him to establish touch with B.H.Q. and 3rd Regiment in anticipation "of my arrival. At the same time I ordered 1 troop of Regimental Re-"serve, under Lt. W. K. King, M.C. to occupy the Tellul Right No. 1 "and to delay the enemy in conjunction with Bluff Posts, till the 1st "Regiment, the Brigade Reserve, got there.

"At 0310 Vale Post reported they were being heavily pressed and "I ordered the garrison (1 troop 3rd Regiment) back to their 2nd position Abu Telluln Left No.1, where they came under order of their "own C/O. At 0320 the enemy poured through the Vale Post and I with-"drew with the Regimental Staff and details to Abu Tellul Right No. 3.

"By this time Mussallabeh was being attacked heavily; the enemy "succeeded in cutting the wire opposite No. 4 Post and temporarily "bombed the occupants out. An immediate counter attack organised by "Sergt. Carlyon, M.M., ejected them.

"The enemy was not able to make any impression on posts 1, 2, "and 3 and when day dawned these posts were able to reverse their fire, "inflicting heavy casualties on the enemy on Bluff and Abu Tellul Right "and very materially assisting the 1st Regiment in the subsequent "counter attack. Vyse Post, to which the garrison of Vance Post had "withdrawn about 0230, held up the direct advance of the enemy but "it was very soon completely surrounded, for as above stated the enemy "poured through the gap at Vale Post. The Vyse Post garrison also "reversed most of its fire at daylight and inflicted heavy casualties "on the enemy in Wadi Dhib and Abu Tellul, causing the enemy to "retire in disorder when the counter attack was launched. As this "post was threatened I left one troop of my reserve attached to Major "Brown. Maskerah was now threatened from the rear and not being "suitable to defend from that direction Capt. Evans, M.C., wisely moved "the garrison to another position prepared for such an eventuality "and was thus able to bring fire to bear on the Bluff, greatly assist-"ing the small party there and very materially assisting in the counter "attack. The enemy attempted to advance down the flat north of "Maskerah at 0600 but were dispersed by fire from that post.

"To revert the position on Bluff and Abu Tellul Right, which were "beyond doubt the key to the situation, at 0330 the Bluff was held by "one troop of "B" Squadron under Lieut. Henderson—No. 1 Abu Tellul "was held by one troop of "A" Squadron, under Lieut W. K. King, M.C. "(thus accounting for the balance of the Regimental Reserve) Nos. "2 and 3 Abu Tellul were held by Regimental Staff and a handful of "Details. These positions were obviously of vital importance, as even "temporary possession of them by the enemy would have meant "the putting out of action, if not the capturing, of the three batteries "situated immediately to the south of Abu Tellul. Further, had the "ridge been taken by the enemy, it is doubtful whether the 1st "Regiment would have been strong enough to retake it, and in the "meantime right flank of the 3rd Regiment would have been seriously "threatened. My instructions to the troops holding them therefore, "were to hold them at all costs till the 1st Regiment could come up.

"The enemy attacked all three posts—employing over 1000 men—
"under cover of heavy and accurate shell fire. Lieut. King, M.C., put
"up a most heroic defence, but was overwhelmed greatly by superior
"numbers. He was killed and every man of his troop either killed
"or wounded.

"Lieut Henderson also put up a gallant performance. He was
"wounded and his troop reduced to three men, but with these he held
"the Bluff against great odds, till the counter attack relieved him.

"Abu Tellul Nos. 2 and 3 were also heavily attacked and we were
"forced out of No. 2 by superior numbers.

"The crest of the ridge and No. 3 were held till two squadrons of the
"1st Regiment arrived shortly after 0500. Thus they were able to get on
"to the ridge without casualties, and were able to develop their counter
"attack from an advantageous position. For nearly two hours this
"handful of men (under Lieuts. G. T. Pledger, Adjutant; Wright, act-
"ing Signal Officer, and Sinton, Assistant Adjutant) were the only troops
"between the Germans and the batteries, watering areas etc. Owing
"to my Signal Sergeant (whom I sent back early in the fight to
"get me in touch with Brigade from Abu Tellul) having become a
"casualty after he left me I had no direct touch—but again reported
"the situation to Brigade Major from 3rd Regiment H.Q. about 0430.
"When the sun rose I got visual touch.

"On arrival of two squadrons of 1st Regiment under Major Weir
"I immediately ordered him to counter attack and arranged covering
"fire for him by the garrison of Abu Tellul. No. 1 (3rd Regiment)
"my own Regimental details and 2 M.G. under Capt. Hackney. With
"this support Major Weir made a brilliant counter attack, forcing the
"Germans under concentrated fire of my posts at Vyse, Mussallabeh
"and Maskerah.

"The fact that Lieut Henderson was still holding portion of the
"Bluff also assisted materially. By 0900 the whole of the position
"was again in our hands, the enemy having suffered very heavily.
"Heavy casualties were inflicted on them outside our wire by the
"artillery, M.G. and rifle fire—these can only be estimated as they were
"able to move them.

"The known casualties, however, were: Killed, 55; wounded, 45;
"prisoners, 330. We collected 15 automatic rifles, 1 M.G., and 130 rifles
"The performance was one of the best the Regiment ever put up—every
"man doing his duty efficiently under most strenuous circumstances.
"The heroic sacrifices of Lieut. King and his troop deserve special
"notice. The gallant and stubborn resistance of Lieut. Henderson and
"his troop rank amongst the best of the Regiment's performances.
"The steadiness of the three main posts and the able manner in which
"they were handled by their commanders (Major W. J. Brown, Capt.
"M. D. McDougal and Capt. F. Evans, M.C.) were exemplary. The
"manner in which the Regimental details, under Lieuts. Pledger, Sin-
"ton and Wright, held their critical posts is also worthy of the highest
"praise—the complete success of the engagements being obviously

"due in a great measure to the fact that the key to the position was "denied to the enemy till the Reserve Regiment arrived.

"Our casualties though serious were very light considering the "severity of the operation."

July 15, 1918.

The 15th July was employed in burying enemy dead and in collecting the captured material. Enemy parites also, under cover of the Red Cross, came out and collected their dead and wounded, beyond our wire. The following day our positions, and especially the horse lines, were heavily shelled for two hours, Captain Handley, Farrier Sergeant Chambers and three others being killed. We spent the day repairing trenches and wire that had been knocked about. At 2350 that night, we were relieved by the 8th Light Regt., and were ordered out of the Jordan Valley for a rest. On 17th the regiment vice Lt.-Col. Bourne who was temporarily in command of the Brigade inspected on 18th by the Corp. Commander (Lt. General Sir Harry Chauvel) who congratulated us on the operation just concluded. On 19th we continued through Jerusalem to Arrub, reaching the latter on the 20th.

On 21st 30 men, under Major Brown, were sent to Port Said on leave. On 22nd B. Squadron, under Major Franklin returned to Jerusalem on a three days tour of duty as Town Picquet. Two officers and 32 men proceeded to Bethlehem for same period, on similar duty.

On 24th July the regiment started for Wady Hanein, where we arrived on 26th. It was a treat to be again on the pleasant and fertile plains, after the Jordan Valley, and the stony hills about Jerusalem. During the spell here, it was possible for one squadron at a time to go to the beach for a swim which was much appreciated.

On 31st July the Brigade was reviewed by the Commander-in-Chief, General Sir Edmund Allenby. Major Birbeck was in charge of the Regiment vice Lt.-Col. Bourne who was temporarily in command of the Brigade This was our first mounted ceremonial parade since Sir Ian Hamilton inspected us early in 1915. General Allenby addressed the Brigade in highly complimentary terms, speaking of our work throughout the campaign. He was specially pleased with our performance at Mussallabeh and Abu Tellul. After the address, the Brigade marched past in column of troops, General Allenby taking the salute.

The following fortnight was spent in N.C.O.'s classes, Hotchkiss gun classes, etc., dubbing saddlery, etc. This work was varied by a couple of sports meetings and by occasional trips to the beach for a swim.

CHAPTER IX

THE LAST PHASE

ON August 16 we received orders to return to the Jordan Valley and we marched with the Brigade at 0700 on the 17th, halting and bivouacing at Latron, Enab, Bethany and Kilo 17. We arrived in the Valley on 21st and next day took over Vale, View, Vaux, Zoo, Zeiss and Zerum Posts from 10th L.H. Regt. Each post was held by one N.C.O. and 9 men in conjunction with detachments of the British West Indian Regt (the Black Anzacs), who were now employed in the front line for the first time. They were particularly keen and intelligent. The sector was very quiet at this time.

On 27th Major Stodart assumed command of the Regt. vice Lt.-Col· Bourne evacuated with malaria. Beyond intermittent shelling of our positions, there was little excitement till 30th when a patrol under Lieut. Joyner was sent out west of Vaux and Wood Posts to search for tracks suitable for wheeled traffic, in anticipation of an advance by us northwards up the Jordan Valley. Lt. Joyner reported the country very broken and unsuitable for wheels. His patrol was shelled the whole time it was out, but suffered no casualty.

On 5th September we were relieved by the Wellington Mounted Rifles and moved into bivouac. Signs of the coming big offensive were now in evidence. Troops were being moved from the Jordan Valley each night. Those remaining in the Valley were ordered to make as much movement and dust during daylight as possible. Everything was done to induce the enemy to believe that the attack would be launched from our right flank. Vacated camps in the Valley were left standing, and even dummy horses were constructed to deceive the enemy airmen.

On 15th September our B. Squadron, under Major Franklin, was detailed as escort to the Corps Commander, Lieutenant General Sir Harry Chauvel, whose headquarters had been moved to Sarona. The squadron marched out with its transport the same day. Chapter 10 contains their narrative while detached. For the previous fortnight, the regiment had been firing Hotchkiss gun courses, and training additional gunners, etc. The number of men attacked by malaria was very large, and specialists such as signallers and Hotchkiss gunners, had to be trained in excess of the establishments, to provide for casualties. On 18th September orders were received to form a dump of certain stores and equipment which would interfere with our mobility.

On 19th September we were advised that a mixed force (to be known as Chaytor's Force) had been formed under our Divisional Commander, Major General Sir E. W. C. Chaytor, to operate on the right flank, viz., the Eastern end of the British line. The force consisted of the A.N.Z.A.C. Division (less our B Squadron), five batteries of Artillery, Detachment of Engineers, two Battalions West Indian Regiment, two Battalions Royal Fusiliers (Jewish) and an Indian Brigade. In the subsequent operations the 1st Light

Horse Brigade was General Chaytor's Reserve, and the 2nd Regiment, owing to its greatly reduced strength, was Brigade Reserve.

On 20th September we received orders to be ready to move at a moment's notice. The West Indians opened the ball by capturing Baker and Chalk Ridges and Grant Hill, while the New Zealand Mounted Rifles seized Kh. Fusail.

On 21st A. Squadron, under Major Brown was sent to support the West Indians and to connect their right with the left of the Fusiliers.. On 22nd the Regiment moved to Kh Fusial and took up a line to protect the rear of the New Zealand Brigade which was attacking the bridge at Jisr-ed-Damieh. The enemy by this time became aware of the complete overthrow of his right flank (see Chapter 10) and his anxiety to make good his escape northwards naturally meant that his resistence to our advance was much less stubborn than we had previously experienced. On 23rd with the rest of 1st Brigade, we attacked and captured Mafid Jozelah. At the same time the 2nd Brigade captured Kabr Mujahid and the New Zealanders pushed on into Es Salt. The advance was continued on 24th, and next day the Aucklands cut the enemy railway at Zuka while the 1st and 2nd Light Horse Brigades and balance of New Zealand Brigade captured Amman.

On 26th September we occupied Wadi el Hamman—the 1st Light Horse Brigade taking 300 prisoners there. On 29th the enemy garrison of Maan, endeavoring to escape northwards, encountered the 5th Light Horse Regiment; and finding they were completely cut off, surrendered at El Kastal. This was the biggest bag of prisoners yet taken by the Division—over 4000 men were captured, and three batteries of guns. On 30th September our A. Squadron was ordered to occupy Suweileh and on 5th October the balance of the Regiment moved to that village, and billeted in the Circassian huts. Our duty was to find patrols to the villages of An-es-Sir, and Rumemin, and keep the district quiet and the roads open. There were still enemy detachments in the mountains, though they were now without supplies. That portion of the enemy left flank which had escaped being cut off, was in full retreat to Deraa and Damascus, and was being dealt with by the other Divisions of Descorps as will be related later.

On 15th October Lieutenant Colonel Bourne returned from hospital and resumed command of the Regiment. Patrols and routine work occupied the next few days. Malaria had by now made such ravages that the Regiment had only one man to three horses. The other units were not much better off. The mounted troops of Chaytor's force (less 2nd Light Horse Regiment) were at Amman, and the infantry had returned to Jerusalem to relieve the strain on the supply columns. So far as our flank was concerned, the fighting was over.

On 28th October there was a Ceremonial Parade at which all units of the A.N.Z.A.C. Division were represented, on the occasion of the hoisting of the Hejaz Flag at Amman. One of the conditions of the co-operation of the King of the Hejaz had been that the district (and a good deal more) was to be given to him. On 30th October the 2nd and 3rd Regiments were reviewed by Gaafar Pasha (a Hejaz officer) with General Chaytor. Gaafar Pasha had the unique distinction of wearing the Iron Cross and the C.M.G.—the former was won when he was fighting with the Turks—the latter was awarded by the British authorities for his subsequent services under the King of the Hejaz our ally. This week was memorable for a splendid consignment of Comforts Fund goods which reached us—the first for many weeks.

On 31st October the Armistice with Turkey was concluded and Chaytor's Force, less 2nd and 3rd Light Horse Regiments marched from Amman, en route to Jerusalem. The operations of General Chaytor's Force in this final phase, resulted in the capture of over 10,000 prisoners, many guns, machine guns, etc., and a great quantity of valuable railway rolling stock.

But this was only part of the bag. The victory was perhaps the most complete recorded in history, and was a wonderful tribute to the Commander-in-Chief (now Lord Allenby, of Megiddo) and his staff. Within four weeks of the commencement of the offensive, the three Turkish armies had been annihilated. No less than 75,000 prisoners had been taken in all, including 3700 Germans and Austrians, 360 guns, 800 machine guns, 210 motor lorries, 50 motor cars, 90 railway engines, 470 trucks and 3500 transport animals (vide Gullett's official history).

Our A squadron, under Captain McLean moved to Amman on 31st October to act as covering party for details engaged in salvage of enemy material (guns, motor lorries, railway rolling stock, etc.)

On 2nd November the 2nd and 3rd Regiments (less A. Squadron, 2nd Regiment) marched via Es Salt to Nimrin, en route for Jerusalem. Our Regiment went into bivouac on the outskirts of that city, the remainder of the Brigade proceeding to Rafa. Owing to the withdrawal of a large proportion of troops to the coast, there were plenty of tents, etc., and we soon made a very comfortable camp. The weather was now cold in the Judean Hills, sleet and frosts were common. Opportunities were freely availed of by all ranks, to visit Holy Places at Jerusalem and Bethlehem. One party visited the latter place and attended the midnight service in the Church of Nativity, on Christmas eve..

On 12th November Major Birkbeck assumed command of the Regiment on the C.O. proceeding to Rafa to take charge of the Brigade. December and January were devoted to cleaning equipment in anticipation of early demobilisation, classes under the Repatriation Educational scheme, and sports meetings. We sent a team to Rafa to compete in the Divisional football tournament and athletic meeting.

On 1st January, 1919, our B Squadron returned after its tour of duty with Corps H.Q., particulars of which will be given later.

On 30th January the first step of demobilisation commenced. Original members of the Regiment who had urgent business or family reasons, were given the opportunity to return at once to Australia, and 24 men elected to go. Before marching out they were paraded and thanked by the C.O. for their excellent service. The rest of the Regiment cheered them heartily as they moved out.

On 13th February we received orders to destroy all horses over eight years' old. This was a very sad duty. The horses were all in the pink of condition, and it went very much against the grain to shoot them—many of them had covered fully 10,000 miles during the campaign. However, to continue to feed them, when their usefulness had passed, was waste of public money, and after all, we preferred that our old friends should die, than that they should be sold to the local residents.

This week we were given a new "toast," viz., "Home Soon." This was given by Col. (Chaplain) Garland of the Church of England Comforts Fund, who visited us to ascertain what we required in the way of books, stationery, etc., for our Repatriation Educational classes. He brought welcome news of embarkation for home at a comparatively early date; and subsequently sent us a useful consignment of school-room material. Classes were held as follows: Elementary Electricity, Internal Construction Engines, Blacksmithing, Reading, Writing and Arithmetic. We were much indebted to the instructors, Lieut. Wills (Signalling Officer), the Farrier Q.M.S. and Padre Ure, who made the classes very interesting to students. A captured German car was used for demonstration purposes.

CHAPTER X

SYRIA—"B" SQUADRON, WITH CORPS H.Q.

THE A.N.Z.A.C. Mounted Division had had most of the fighting from the beginning of the Sinai-Palestine-Syria campaign; but this did not prevent keen disappointment when it became known that its role in the final operations, though highly important, was secondary to that of the rest of Desert Corps, which in the next few weeks was to bound from Ludd to Nazareth and Tiberias, to Damascus and Beirut, to Homs and Aleppo—no less than 350 miles as the crow flies. The Regiment, of course, shared in the disappointment of the Division, but our B Squadron, in being detailed as escort to the Corps Commander, certainly "drew a prize." As already noted the Squadron was detached from the Regiment on 15th September and reached Corps H.Q. at Sarona by three night marches. As mobility was to be a main factor in the operations, the weight to be carried by horses was reduced to the minimum. Though the weather was getting cold, and we expected to be in the mountains of Lebanon, we had to leave our great coats behind, and started out with one blanket, one oil sheet and one spare pair of socks per man. When it is remembered that we had only just come from the Jordan Valley 1200 feet below sea level, and expected to reach snow level in the next few weeks, it will be realised that we were going to feel the change.

Before dawn on 19th September our guns opened fire on the sector of enemy trenches nearest the sea. It was by far the heaviest artillery fire we had heard—no less than 300 guns having been concentrated for the attack. The enemy were completely surprised, having expected us to advance against their other flank, and our four Divisions of Infantry which assaulted the Tabsor and adjoining trench system the moment the guns lifted, were successful at all points. Our cavalry, 20,000 strong crossed the old Turkish trenches shortly after dawn; and then began the race northwards, which was to tax the fitness of men and horses to the uttermost. Over the open country, we swept, reaching Liktera (on the coast 25 miles from starting point) by 1100. It was amazing to find that after the first enemy line was crossed, there were no other redoubts in rear, and no reserves camped, which proved that our bluff of attacking up the Jordan Valley, had completely misled the Turks.

From Liktera we swung to the East, to cut the communications of the Turkish 3rd Corps north of Nablus. Pushing through the Mus-Mus Pass on the 20th September, we saw Indian Lancers on the Plain of Esdraelon charge a Turkish column which was marching up to hold the Pass. The Corps Commander decided to make his headquarters at Megiddo; and here, we halted for seven days while the three Divisions spread out fanwise to Nazareth Beisan and Jenin. Prisoners began to stream in, and guard duties to multiply for the Escort Squadron. The second night three Turks, wishing to surrender, wandered into the Corps Commander's tent. Next night we had to provide another sentry!

The news which reached us daily was most thrilling. The rapidity of the advance had prevented serious opposition to the Cavalry Divisions, which were covering on an average about 60 miles per day. The Infantry Divisions, on the other hand, were having very stiff fighting, though the capture of Tulkeram and Nablus by General Onslow's Brigade, had given them great assistance. The brilliant capture of Jenin with over 8000 prisoners, by General Wilson's Brigade followed.

By the fourth day we were guarding 12,000 prisoners with two troops. Half the squadron had already been sent back with 4000. Many prisoners having marched from Jenin, were nearly mad with thirst; and we marched them down in batches to canvas troughs where they buried their heads in the water. Some filled their boots with water to take back to the compound with them.

On 22nd September Haifa was captured. By 24th September the magnitude of the victory began to be apparent, two enemy Army Corps having been annihilated. On 25th September, our friends, the 11th Light Horse Regiment had a very stiff fight at Samakh, on the shores of the Sea of Gallilee, which they captured. Corps. H.Q. was now at Nazareth, a pretty little village of white wailed, red roofed houses, perched in a hollow, high up in the hills. Here we began to taste the fruits of victory, in the shape of rare brands of champagne, and excellent cigars, which had once been the property of a Hun officer's Mess. We began to view life through rose colored glasses.

On 26th September orders to advance on Damascus were issued, and we marched to Tiberias which had just been captured by the 3rd Light Horse Brigade. Imagine a column of dusty horseman finding at their feet the beautiful blue sea of Gallilee. Horse and man went straight in for a very necessary bath. Next evening we pushed on to Jisr-Benat-Yakub (Bridge of Jacobs Daughters) where we had a few hours sleep. We crossed the Jordan next morning and climbed to Kuneitra, where we were ordered to fill water bottles and prepare for a 40 mile dash to Damascus. Every possible position of vantage en route was defended by well posted German machine gunners, whose stubborn opposition greatly delayed our march, so that the morning was well advanced when we came in sight of Damascus. Abandoned enemy motor cars, lorries, guns, etc strewed the road.

Our troops practically surrounded Damascus, General Wilson's Brigade actually galloping through it; but the honor of officially "capturing" it was reeserved for political reasons, for the Sherifian force, which entered next morning. They took 3000 prisoners in the City while our troop bagged 20,000.

This wonderful old city is situated on the fertile plain at the foot of the Barada Gorge. TheBarada and Barbar Rivers are the Biblical Abana and Pharpar—the "Rivers of Damascus."

The former rushing down from the Lebanons, furnishes hydro-electric power for Damascus trams, lighting and industries. Before the stream reaches the city it is divided into seven canals, which irrigate the beautiful gardens. Some fine buildings ornament the city too; but in its present appaling condition, its natural beauty was quite lost. Apart from the 20,000 prisoners who now had to be fed and cared for, the hospitals were crowded to an unbelievable extent. Dead and dying Turks lay in the streets. Three thousand Armenian children who had been brought by the Turks to Damascus were starving, and required immediate attention. Malaria spread rapidly among our own troops as well as the Turks, and we lost Sergt. Paddy Linan and Trooper Sinclair here. Dysentery, typhus and cholera were taking heavy toll of Turks and civilians. The streets of Damascus were thronged daily with long haired, wild looking Arabs—Allies of whom we were hardly proud, they had let us down so often. They persisted in firing their rifles off into the air, to show their joy or else to let us see that they really knew how to do it. They caused some deaths among the civil population.

The question on the lips of all civilians was: "Who is to govern the country?" "Under whose rule will we now live? English, French or Sherifian?" The Christian element openly stated that thy would prefer Turkish to Sherifian rule. We spent a month at Damascus while the Mounted Divisions cleaned up the enemy in Aleppo, Rayak and Beirut. On 29th October we moved out on a 100 mile trek to Homs. On arrival there on 1st November we received news of the Armistice which had been signed on terms dictated by our Commander-in-Chief.

On 23rd December we handed our horses over to the 5th Cavalry Division. It was hard to part from these tried old friends, but it was inevitable, as we were to rejoin the Regiment at Jerusalem, by train. On 24th December the drought broke—or in other words, the A.I.F. Canteen managed to get a supply of beer up to us ! We entrained on Christmas Day, and passing through the wonderful ruins of Baal-Bik, Damascus and Haifa, rejoined the regiment in Jerusalem on 1st January, 1919, the dawn of a New Year of Peace!

CHAPTER XI

HOME SOON

ON February 23 we handed all rifles and equipment into Ordnance stores. A memorial service for fallen comrades was held at St. George's Cathedral, Jerusalem, which the whole Regiment attended. The remaining horses left next day, under Major Birkbeck, to be handed over to the Remount Section, Moascar. On 25th February we left Jerusalem by train, arriving at Rafa at 0400 on 26th. Here we rejoined the Brigade which was awaiting orders to embark.

On 10th March Major General Chaytor made his final inspection of the Regiment, thanked us for our services throughout the campaign, and said good bye. On 12th March we entrained for Kantara and next day embarked, together with some 1st Brigade details and the 1st Light Horse Regiment, on H.M.T. "Ulimaroa." The voyage home was uneventful—physical training and sports meetings employed most of our time. We were splendidly fed on the voyage; and thanks to a generous donation by Mrs. Chisholm and Miss McPhillamy, from the profits made by their excellent canteen, we were provided with fruit, etc., at ports en route. We had short leave on 26th March at Colombo. Major Franklin was disembarked here to go into hospital. He reached Sydney two months later, but died in the Military Hospital there. His keen interest in the welfare of his men had earned him their sincere regard. There was something singularly pathetic about the deaths of those who, having survived the dangers of active service, reached home, but were robbed of the joy of reunion with their friends.

On 7th April we arrived at Fremantle, where we were suprised to learn that we were supposed to be suffering from pneumonic influenza. As a matter of fact there had been very little sickness during the voyage and no influenza. The quarantine officers inspected every man, and daily inspections were carried out by our own medical officers during the remainder of the voyage. There was a further inspection at Albany, and again at Melbourne, where we arrived on 16th. Here we dropped two officers and 17 other ranks, whose homes were in Victoria. On 18th we arrived in Sydney harbour and the ship was promptly sent into quarantine for four days. On 21st we disembarked 40 men who came from the Northern Rivers of New South Wales.

On 23rd we arrived in Moreton Bay and to our disgust were sent into quarantine camp at Lytton· The idea that we might be bringing pneumonic influenza into the country was dying hard. Conditions at Lytton would have been uncomfortable had it not been for the efforts of the ladies' committee of the Regimental Comforts Fund who sent fruit, etc., to us. Our best thanks are due to that committee which had worked hard throughout the war to send us regular consignments of comforts, Christmas billies, etc.

On 30th April we arrived in Brisbane. We had the honor of being in-

75

vited to march through the streets as a unit. The State Governor took the salute at Albert Square, and a guard of honor, under our first C.O. Colonel Stodart, and composed of returned men of the Regiment, was formed up at the saluting base. We dismissed at the drill hall, Adelaide Street. The same afternoon the Regimental colors were deposited in St. John's Cathedral, following century old precedent.

CONCLUSION

THAT 30th April, 1919, when we ceased to exist as a Regiment, seems a long way off. How glad we were to get home! But is there one of us who, looking back, does not find pleasure in recalling the old days in the A.I.F.—the splendid friendships formed; the trials, hardships, and perils shared; great difficulties overcome; a victory more complete than any in History, won? The consciousness that we had the good fortune to be of an age that permitted us to share in the "Birth of our Nation"—that baptism of blood on Gallipoli, will be valued more and more as we grow older. How many of us will serve with a Mounted Regiment again? How many will long to hear the Trumpet calls? "Stables," "Feed up," and then the music of the neighing of 600 horses, changed in a few seconds, as their nose bags are put on, to a contented munching?

There was something fascinating about those old days in spite of all. There is something that makes those friendships then formed, more precious than we can say. May they last while life lasts—and may the spirit of the A.I.F., the spirit of Anzac, last in our children and in their children, that Australia may be honoured throughout the world.

APPENDIX

During the War there passed through the Regiment—

Officers 103
Other Ranks 2508

Summary of Casualties

Killed 201
Wounded 458

The following made the supreme sacrifice :—

Number	Rank	Name	Date
292	Trooper . . .	Arthur, L. R.	7/8/15
293	Trooper . . .	Alexander, C. B.	7/4/15
459	Corporal . . .	Alexander, J. C.	14/5/15
596	Trooper . . .	Anderson, A. E.	15/5/15
611	Trooper . . .	Adams, W. H.	14/5/15
755	Trooper . . .	Anderson, A.	7/8/15
927	Trooper . . .	Allen, F. C.	11/11/15
962	L. Cpl. . . .	Anthony, A. H.	9/1/17
1080	Trooper . . .	Angus, M.	9/1/17
1229	Trooper . . .	Ansell, F.	31/10/17
1307	Trooper . . .	Archibald, R.	3/2/16
1537	Trooper . . .	Arthur, C.	24/11/17
2928	Trooper . . .	Archibald, L. L.	11/4/18
	Lieut.	Burge, J.	7/8/15
96	Sergt.	Barry, H. J.	7/8/15
124	Sergt.	Barnes, J. P.	9/1/17
299	Sergt.	Brown, T. M.	20/4/17
472	Trooper . . .	Burton, A. A.	14/5/15
483	Trooper . . .	Beyers, J. A.	14/5/15
485	Sergt.	Bond, C. J.	30/5/15
592	Trooper . . .	Buchanan, C. G. G. . . .	14/5/15
723	Trooper . . .	Butler, E. R.	14/5/15
1083	Trooper . . .	Boyle, J. J.	12/1/17
1543	Trooper . . .	Bailey, R.	9/1/17
1548	Trooper . . .	Brown, F.	28/3/18
2302	Trooper . . .	Bryce, W.	3/12/17
2868	Trooper . . .	Bunkum, W. E. H. . . .	14/7/18
3349	Trooper . . .	Beck, C.	31/10/17
375	Trooper . . .	Brown, H. S.	28/5/15
	Major	Chambers, A. F.	20/4/17
32	Driver	Carl, W.	7/8/15
134	Sergt.	Cowie, J.	14/7/18
135	Sergt.	Cowley, E. C.	9/1/17
273	S.Q.M.S. . . .	Cartwright, F.	18/4/15
311	Farrier Sergt	Chambers, J. A.	16/7/18
489	Trooper . . .	Crowther, S.	14/5/15
490	Driver	Casey, P.	14/5/15
797	Trooper . . .	Campbell, D. D.	4/8/16
859	L. Cpl.	Cameron, C.	9/1/17

Number	Rank	Name	Date
1400	Trooper . . .	Cunningham, T. A. . . .	4/8/16
1316	Trooper . . .	Cummins, G.	7/11/17
2247	Trooper . . .	Coney, W.	14/7/18
2634	Trooper . . .	Crozier, J. F.	11/1/17
2635	Trooper . . .	Crozier, R. J.	11/4/18
2872	Trooper . . .	Callaghan, P.	19/4/17
3114	Trooper . . .	Cooper, R.	27/3/18
3175	Trooper . . .	Cornick, G. F.	14/7/18
3414	Trooper . . .	Collett, P. P.	11/4/18
3471	Trooper . . .	Cain, M. W.	18/10/18
3479A	Trooper . . .	de Crespigny, P. C. . . .	14/7/18
745	Corporal . . .	Cochrane, J. W.	20/7/15
142	Trooper . . .	Day, A.	11/2/17 (While prisoner of War)
312	Trooper . . .	Demmick, L.	3/3/16
461	Sergt.	Drysdale, G. R.	11/2/17 (While prisoner of War)
504	Trooper . . .	Davies, T.	14/5/15
618	Trooper . . .	Denton, V.	31/5/15
735	Trooper . . .	Durham, G. T.	31/10/17
741	Trooper . . .	Dwyer, J. T.	7/8/15
1155	Trooper . . .	Davies, W. J.	22/12/17
1241	Trooper . . .	De Raadt, J. L. C. . . .	17/10/15
1304	Trooper . . .	Dinsdale, T. S.	1/11/17
2165	Trooper . . .	Daniels, W. E.	11/4/18
2329	Trooper . . .	Dale, T.	4/8/16
2994	Trooper . . .	Deberg, A. H.	14/7/18
317	L. Cpl. . . .	Easton, F P.	19/11/16 (While prisoner of War)
646	Corporal . . .	Emerson, J. E. R. . . .	11/4/18
805	Sergt.	Ellis, H. V. V.	22/10/18
1160	Trooper . . .	Elliott, W.	17/7/18
150	Trumpeter .	Foote, N. V.	7/4/15
311A	Sergt.	Floyd, L. L.	8/3/18
601	Trooper . . .	Faircloth, B.	14/7/18
1018	Trooper . . .	Finnis, P. W.	4/8/16
2877	Corporal . . .	Fisher, C. H.	9/1/17
	Major	Graham, D. M. L. . . .	14/5/15
155	Sergt.	Geddes, (M.M.), J. R. .	14/7/18
328	Trooper . . .	Geoghegan, A. M. C. .	15/9/15
462	Corporal . . .	Graffunder, A. C. J. . .	14/5/15
514	Trooper . . .	Garvey, L. P.	14/5/15
517	Trooper . . .	Goodall, T. L.	14/5/15
772	Trooper . . .	Gibbs, S. J.	21/7/16
1091	Sergt.	Grau, F. W.	14/7/18
1421	Trooper . . .	Gwynne, T. K.	2/11/18
3239	Trooper . . .	Grieve, C. J.	16/7/18
	Capt.	Handley, W. J.	16/7/18
	Lieut.	Hinton, H. G.	7/8/15
160	Trooper . . .	Harman, H.	2/8/15
523	Trooper . . .	Hannah, J.	14/5/15
529	Trooper . . .	Hulbert, P. R.	18/7/15
624	Trooper . . .	Harris, O.	17/5/15

Number	Rank	Name	Date
771	Trooper ...	Hammond, H.	7/8/15
869	Trooper ...	Hamp, S. S.	7/8/15
1003	Trooper ...	Harte, M. A.	3/1/16
1094	Corporal ...	Hanslow, N.	22/4/17
2809A	Trooper ...	Haigh, C. W.	6/11/18
2999	Trooper ...	Hildebrand, T. W. ...	14/7/18
3240	Trooper ...	Irish, V. C.	14/7/18
169	Trooper ...	Jury, M. V.	25/8/15
1029	Trooper ...	Jones, T.	6/12/15
	Lieut.	Kemp, A. C.	14/4/18
	Lieut.	King, (M.C.), W. K. ..	14/7/18
170	Trooper ...	Keid, W.	23/6/15
340	Trooper ...	Kerr, J.	29/6/15
341	Trooper ...	Kimber, J. H.	7/5/15
342	Trooper ...	Kelly, J. A.	17/5/16
1227	Trooper ...	Kirk, A. C.	11/4/18
1248	Trooper ...	Kelsall, J.	4/11/17
2146	Trooper ...	Kennett, V. I. N.	9/2/17
		(While prisoner of War)	
	Major	Logan, Thos.	7/8/15
	Lieut.	Letch, H. A.	22/8/18
		(With Flying Corps)	
103	Sergt.	Linnan, P. P.	4/11/18
247	Trooper ...	Lush, J. R.	7/8/15
780	Corporal ...	Langridge, T. E. ...	18/5/17
882	Trooper ...	Lord, A. C.	6/12/15
1100	Corporal ...	Larkin, S. C.	28/10/18
3300	Trooper ...	Loman, T. A.	30/7/18
	Major	Markwell, D.S.O., W.E.	31/10/17
17	Trooper ...	Mouritz, L. B.	14/5/15
21	Driver	McDonald, A.	2/11/17
74	Driver	McCreedy, R.	16/11/15
176	Signaller ..	McAllister, W. J. A. ..	24/5/15
179	Trooper ...	McGowan, E.	22/5/15
180	Trooper ...	McNamara, L.	20/5/15
234	Trooper ...	Masters, G. A. L. ...	5/7/15
241	Trooper ...	McMahon, J. P.	15/3/16
347	Trooper ...	Marson, C.	7/8/15
348	Trooper ...	Moran, W. G.	29/6/15
352	Sergt.	Matthews, A.	9/1/17
356	Corporal ...	Masters, S. G.	14/7/18
358	Trooper ...	Macfarlane, C. J. ...	3/7/15
538	Trooper ...	McIndoe, E. J.	5/6/15
541	L. Cpl. ...	Mulvey, F. C.	14/5/15
545	Trooper ...	Martin, G. B.	1/11/17
600	Trooper ...	Murray, D.	17/6/15
786	Trooper ...	McKinnon, D.	15/12/15
787	Trooper ...	Milford, W.	11/8/15
888	Trooper ...	McMartin, A. G.	1/11/17
952	Trooper ...	Marks, W. L.	11/4/18
1105	Trooper ...	McLean, H. A.	3/12/15

Number	Rank	Name	Date
1182	Trooper . . .	Morgan, J. A.	14/8/16
1628	Trooper . . .	McCann, W. E.	11/4/16
	Major	Nash, A. W.	29/6/15
366	Trooper . . .	Norton, W. T.	19/6/15
1721	Corporal . . .	Nash, I. T.	5/3/16
370	Trooper . .	O'Connor, W. H.	19/6/15
423	Trooper . . .	Ogilvy, J.	2/8/15
557	Sergt.	Oswin, A. E.	14/5/15
945	Trooper . . .	O'Leary, J.	11/11/15
2477	Trooper . . .	O'Callaghan, T.	4/8/16
3287	Corporal . . .	Ogg, T. A.	14/7/18
3250	Trooper . . .	O'Connor, L.	16/7/18
95	Farrier Sergt	Pickering, A.	10/12/17
190	Trooper . . .	Pearce, E. C. W.	7/8/15
198	Trooper . . .	Parker, K. A.	20/4/15
199	Trooper . . .	Phillips, T. H.	14/5/15
719	Trooper . . .	Perrott, H. J.	12/10/15
1111	Trooper . . .	Peterson, E.	3/11/15
1261	Trooper . . .	Perkins, T. O.	11/4/18
1341	Trooper . . .	Parkes, W. J.	9/8/16
3491	Trooper . . .	Peach, W. J.	14/7/18
201	Trooper . . .	Quinn, J. W.	22/12/15
	Lieut.	Righetti, A. S.	4/8/16
378	Trooper . . .	Robertson, G. H.	13/5/15
382	Trooper . . .	Ross, J. R.	9/9/15
383	Trooper . . .	Reade, C. M.	30/5/15
1688	Trooper . . .	Robertson, F. J. K. . .	9/1/17
	Lieut.	Sinclair, D. H. M. . . .	20/4/17
	Lieut.	Swanston, W.	1/11/17
33	Driver	Sefton, R. H.	11/11/15
214	S.Q.M.S. . .	Stewart, H. J.	3/9/15
388	Trooper . . .	Sinclair, H.	15/10/18
593	Trooper . . .	Sims, J. C.	14/5/15
713	Trooper . . .	Stower, R. W.	31/10/17
794	Trooper . . .	Smale, W. E.	7/8/15
795	Trooper . . .	Sharpe, W.	13/8/15
891	Trooper . . .	Stevenson, T.	26/9/15
1046	Trooper . . .	Spry, M.	16/11/15
1266	L. Cpl. . . .	Somerville, J.	10/4/17
		(While prisoner of War)	
1732	Trooper . . .	Sullivan, G.	4/8/16
2218	Trooper . . .	Sullivan, J.	1/11/18
2388	Trooper . . .	Sweedman, E. C. . . .	15/7/18
4052A	Trooper . . .	Sullings, H. A.	31/10/17
570	Trooper . . .	Templer, F. D.	22/10/15
571	Trooper . . .	Tallentire, W. J.	14/5/15
1049	Trooper . . .	Toohey, W.	4/8/16
2381	L. Cpl. . . .	Underwood, T.	22/1/17
645	Trooper . . .	Underhill, R. M.	14/5/15

Number	Rank	Name	Date
	Lieut.	Woodyatt, P. S. R. . .	4/8/16
230	L. Cpl. . . .	Wilson, G. L.	19/5/15
236	Driver	Whittall, P. G.	7/8/15
399	Corporal . . .	Waddell, G. M.	23/12/16
456	Sergt.	Wade, J. S.	14/5/15
584	Trooper . . .	Wentford, J. F. J. . . .	21/5/15
586	Trooper . . .	Wilson, A. G. M. . . .	14/5/15
647	Trooper . . .	Wragge, C. E.	16/5/15
803	Trooper . . .	Wilson, W. T.	7/8/15
804	Trooper . . .	Wylie, E.	9/8/15
973	Trooper . . .	Ward, J. E. N.	6/3/17
			(While prisoner of War)
1117	Trooper . . .	Wallace, A. G.	31/10/17
1121	Trooper . . .	Watt, A. J.	23/12/15
1445	Trooper . . .	Weeks, G. R.	31/10/17
1472	Driver	Wooster, A. C.	2/11/17

THE FOLLOWING DISTINCTIONS WERE GAINED IN THE FIELD

D.S.O.: Lt.-Col. G. H. Bourne, Major G. Birkbeck, Major W. J. Brown, Major R. N. Franklin, Major W. E. Markwell, Major M. Shanahan.

M.C.: Major C. C. Stodart, Capt. Fred Evans, Capt. (Chaplain) H. K. Gordon, Lieut. L. B. Guiren, Lieut. L. J. Henderson, Lieut. W. K. King, Lieut. H. A. Letch, Capt. M. D. McDougall, Lieut. G. T. Pledger, Capt. F. Trinca, Lieut. F. Wilcox.

Medaille Militaire: Lieut. J. Wasson, Trooper W. H. Kenny.

Croix de Guerre: Lieut. J. H. Campbell, Sergt. C. Mowbray.

M.M.: Lieut. J. H. Campbell, Lieut J. M. Wills, Sergt. H. A. Apelt, Sergt. A. F. Biggs, Sergt. J. E. Carlyon, Tpr. C. E. Duff, Cpl. J. E. Emerson, Cpl. T. Finlayson, Sergt. J. R. Geddes, Signaller P. C. Jones, Trooper W. H. Massey, Trooper R. A. Shire, Cpl. G. Volp, Sergt. A. G. Wilson.

D.C.M.: S.S.M. F. J. Ailen, Cpl. A. Baldwin, Trooper W. H. Kenny, Cpl. J. M. McDonald, Trooper F. L. Pringle, Sergt. T. Kirkbride.

Serbian Silver Star: Lieut. R. G. Sinton

Cross of Karra George: Sergt. T. Kirkbride.

A.D.C. to the Governor General: Lt.-Col. G. H. Bourne.

Mentioned in Despatches. Lt.-Col. G. H. Bourne, Major W. E. Markwell (2), Major G. Birkbeck, Major C. C. Stodart, Capt. A. J. Ogilvy, Capt. F. Evans, Capt. H. K. Gordon, Lieut. H. A. Letch, Lieut. J. Wasson, Lieut. F. Wilcox, Lieut. J. M. Wills, Sergt. E. J. A. Cannons, Sergt. J. E. Carlyon, Sergt. J. R. Geddes, Cpl. A. C. J. Graffunder, Trooper W. Keid, Sergt. J. Locke, Sergt. G. O. Morgan, S.S.M. J. A. Menzies, Trooper E. McKee, Sergt. C. Mowbray, Sergt. J. D. Mercer, Sergt. A. E. Oswin, Sergt. G. W. Power, Sergt. J. Pearson, Trooper M. H. Shand, Sergt. J. S. Wade.

Act of Gallantry recorded by G.O.C. Eastern Force: Trooper W. H. Kempson

The following gained Distinctions while seconded from the Regiment, or after transfer to other Units, viz:—

Major-General Sir T. W. Glasgow, K.C.M.G., C.B., D.S.O., Croix de Guerre
Lieut.-Col. T. McSharry, C.M.G., D.S.O., M.C.
Lieut.-Col. G. W. Macartney, D.S.O.
Major Robt. Glasgow, D.S.O., M.C.
Major A. Chisholm, D.S.O.
Major A. E. G. Campbell, D.S.O., M.C.
Capt. Willenbroc, M.C.
Lieut. C. M. McDougall, M.C.

Lieut. E. C. B. Cameron, M.C.
Lieut. E. J. Barton, M.C.
Lieut. W. M. B. Cory, M.C.
Lieut. J. H. Butler, M.C.
Lieut. J. A. Menzies, M.C.
Lieut. R. B. Brown, M.C.
Lieut. Leander Grove, M.C.
Lieut. Nicholson, M.C.
Lieut. Carroll, M.C.
W.O. H. L. A. Frankford, Meritorious Service Medal
Trooper C. J. Tranter, Serbian Gold Medal.

(We regret any possible omissions due to the difficulty of tracing records)

Members of the Regiment will be interested to know that little Jack Hanna who was rescued at Homs by "B" Squadron, ultimately got to Australia. He is anxious to find the men who befriended him.

www.ingramcontent.com/pod-product-compliance
Lightning Source LLC
Chambersburg PA
CBHW080559090426
42735CB00016B/3293